Source Readings in Music History

Source Readings in Music History

SOURCE READINGS IN MUSIC HISTORY

The Renaissance

Selected and Annotated by
OLIVER STRUNK
PRINCETON UNIVERSITY

W · W · NORTON & COMPANY · INC · New York

Musical examples by Gordon Mapes

ISBN 0 393 09681 5

To the Memory of
CARL ENGEL
1883–1944

ABBREVIATIONS

Grad. Vat.	*Graduale . . . de tempore et de sanctis* (Tournai, 1938)
Ant. Vat.	*Antiphonale . . . pro diurnis horis* (Rome, 1912)
	J. P. Migne, *Patrologia cursus completus.*
PL	—*Series latina.* 221 vols. (Paris, 1844–1855)
PG	—*Series graeca.* 166 vols. (Paris, 1857–1866)
GS	Martin Gerbert, *Scriptores ecclesiastici de musica.* 3 vols. (San Blasianis, 1784)
CS	C. E. H. Coussemaker, *Scriptorum de medii aevi nova series.* 4 vols. (Paris, 1864–1876)

Throughout the book, small letters refer to notes by the authors of the individual selections, arabic numerals to editor's notes. The abbreviation "*S.R.*" followed by a Roman numeral refers to another volume in the *Source Readings in Music History.*

Contents

I

MUSICAL THEORISTS OF THE RENAISSANCE

II

MUSIC IN RENAISSANCE LIFE AND THOUGHT

III

REFORMATION AND COUNTER-REFORMATION

Preface to the Five-Volume Edition

My *Source Readings in Music History*, a music-historical companion running to more than 900 pages and extending from classical antiquity through the romantic era, was originally published in 1950. That it is now being reissued in parts is due to a recognition, shared by the publishers and myself, that the usefulness of the book would be considerably enhanced if the readings for the single periods were also available separately and in a handier form. From the first, the aim had been to do justice to every age without giving to any a disproportionate share of the space. Thus the book has lent itself naturally to a division into parts, approximately equal in length, each part complete in itself. For use in the classroom, the advantages of the present edition are sufficiently obvious. For the casual reader, whose interest in the history of music is not likely to be all-inclusive, it will have other advantages, equally obvious. In the meantime, the original edition in one volume will remain in print and will be preferred by those who wish to have the whole between two covers, to be able to refer readily from one part of the book to another, and to be able to consult a single index.

In reprinting here the foreword to the edition of 1950, I have retained only those paragraphs that apply in some measure to all parts of the whole.

O. S.

Rome, 1965

Foreword

THIS BOOK began as an attempt to carry out a suggestion made in 1929 by Carl Engel in his *Views and Reviews*—to fulfil his wish for "a living record of musical personalities, events, conditions, tastes . . . a history of music faithfully and entirely carved from contemporary accounts." It owes something, too, to the well-known compilations of Kinsky and Schering and rather more, perhaps, to Andrea della Corte's *Antologia della storia della musica* and to an evaluation of this, its first model, by Alfred Einstein.

In its present form, however, it is neither the book that Engel asked for nor a literary anthology precisely comparable to the pictorial and musical ones of Kinsky and Schering, still less an English version of its Italian predecessor, with which it no longer has much in common. It departs from Engel's ideal scheme in that it has, at bottom, a practical purpose—to make conveniently accessible to the teacher or student of the history of music those things which he must eventually read. Historical documents being what they are, it inevitably lacks the seemingly unbroken continuity of Kinsky and Schering; at the same time, and for the same reason, it contains far more that is unique and irreplaceable than either of these. Unlike della Corte's book it restricts itself to historical documents as such, excluding the writing of present-day historians; aside from this, it naturally includes more translations, fewer original documents, and while recognizing that the somewhat limited scope of the *Antologia* was wholly appropriate in a book on music addressed to Italian readers, it seeks to take a broader view.

That, at certain moments in its development, music has been a subject of widespread and lively contemporary interest, calling forth a flood of documentation, while at other moments, perhaps not less critical, the records are either silent or unrevealing—this is in no way remarkable, for it is inherent in the very nature of music, of letters, and of history. The beginnings of the classical symphony and string quartet passed virtually unnoticed as developments without interest for the literary man; the beginnings of the opera and cantata, developments which concerned him immediately and deeply, were heralded and reviewed in documents so numerous that, even in a book of this size, it has been possible to include only the most significant. Thus, as already suggested, a documentary history of music cannot properly exhibit even the degree of continuity that is possible for an iconographic one or a collection of musical monuments, still less the degree expected of an interpretation. For this reason, too, I have rejected the simple chronological arrangement as inappropriate and misleading and have preferred to allow the documents to arrange themselves naturally under the various topics chronologically ordered in the Table of Contents and the book itself, some of these admirably precise, others perhaps rather too inclusive. As Engel shrewdly anticipated, the frieze has turned out to be incomplete, and I have left the gaps unfilled, as he wished.

For much the same reason, I have not sought to give the book a spurious unity by imposing upon it a particular point of view. At one time it is the musician himself who has the most revealing thing to say; at another time he lets someone else do the talking for him. And even when the musician speaks it is not always the composer who speaks most clearly; sometimes it is the theorist, at other times the performer. If this means that few readers will find the book uniformly interesting, it ought also to mean that "the changing patterns of life," as Engel called them, will be the more fully and the more faithfully reflected.

It was never my intention to compile a musical Bartlett, and I have accordingly sought, wherever possible, to include the complete text of the selection chosen, or—failing this—the complete text of a continuous, self-contained, and independently intelligible passage or series of passages, with or without regard for the chapter divisions of the original. But in a few cases I have made cuts to eliminate digressions or to avoid needless repetitions of things equally well said by earlier writers; in other cases the excessive length and involved construction of the original has forced me to abridge, reducing the scale of the whole while retaining the essential continuity of the argument. All cuts are clearly indicated, either by a row of dots or in annotations.

Without the lively encouragement and patient sympathy of the late William Warder Norton my work on this book would never have been begun. Nor is it at all likely that I would ever have finished it without the active collaboration of my father, William Strunk, Jr., Emeritus Professor of English at Cornell University, whose expert assistance and sound advice were constantly at my disposal during the earlier stages of its preparation and who continued to follow my work on it with the keenest interest until 1946, the year of his death. A considerable number of

the translations now published for the first time are largely his work
and there are few to which he did not make some improving contribution.

My warmest thanks are due to Professor Otto Kinkeldey, of Cornell
University, and to Professor Alfred Einstein, of Smith College, for their
extraordinary kindness in consenting to read the entire book in proof and
for the many indispensable corrections and suggestions that they have sent
me; again to Alfred Einstein, and to Paul Hindemith, for a number of
constructive recommendations which grew out of their experiments with
sections of the manuscript in connection with their teaching; likewise to
my old friends Paul Lang, Arthur Mendel, and Erich Hertzmann, who
have always been ready to listen and to advise.

Acknowledgment is due, also, to Dr. Dragan Plamenac, who prepared
the greater number of the brief biographical notes which accompany the
single readings; to two of my students—Philip Keppler, Jr., who reliev-
ed me of some part of the proofreading and J. W. Kerman, who prepared
the index; to Gordon Mapes, for his careful work on the autograph-
ing of the musical examples; and to Miss Katherine Barnard, Miss
Florence Williams, and the entire staff of W. W. Norton & Co., Inc.,
for their unflagging interest and innumerable kindnesses.

OLIVER STRUNK

The American Academy in Rome

I

Musical Theorists of the Renaissance

1. Joannes Tinctoris

A native of Flanders, perhaps of Poperinghe, a little town not far from Ypres, Joannes Tinctoris attended the University of Louvain in 1471 and before 1476 had established himself in Naples as chaplain to Ferdinand I (Don Ferrante) and tutor to Beatrice of Aragon, Ferdinand's daughter, afterwards the wife of Matthias Corvinus of Hungary. In 1487 Tinctoris traveled in France and Germany in search of singers for the royal chapel; he died in 1511, a canon of Nivelles. His principal writings include a treatise on the proportions; the *Diffinitorium musices*, our earliest dictionary of musical terms, written for his royal pupil before her marriage in 1476 but not printed until about 1495; a book on the nature and property of the modes, dedicated in 1476 to his distinguished contemporaries Ockeghem and Busnoys; and a book on the art of counterpoint, completed in 1477. Tinctoris is also the composer of a mass on the popular song "L'homme armé" and of a few motets and chansons, some of them printed by Petrucci in his earliest anthologies.

As a theorist, Tinctoris shows little originality. The real interest of his writings lies less in their detailed exposition of technical practices and procedures than in the historical observations with which he embellishes his forewords and in his many references to the works of the great masters of his day, with several of whom he was evidently on friendly terms.

Proportionale musices [1]

[ca. 1476]

The Proportional of Music, by Master Joannes Tinctoris, Licentiate in Laws, Chaplain to the Most Supreme Prince Ferdinand, King of Sicily and Jerusalem, begins with good omen.

---

1 Text: CS, IV, 153b–155a. The treatise may be dated "before 1476," since Tinctoris refers to it in the prologue to his *Liber de natura et pro-* *prietate tonorum* (CS, IV, 16b–17b), completed on November 6, 1476.

DEDICATION

To THE MOST sacred and invincible prince, by the Divine Providence of the King of Kings and Lord of Lords, King of Sicily, Jerusalem, and Hungary, Joannes Tinctoris, the least among professors of music and among his chaplains, proffers humble and slavish obedience, even to kissing his feet.

Although, most wise king, from the time of the proto-musician Jubal, to whom Moses has attributed so much, as when in Genesis he calls him the first of all such as handle the harp and organ,[2] many men of the greatest fame, as David, Ptolemy, and Epaminondas (princes of Judaea, Egypt, and Greece), Zoroaster, Pythagoras, Linus the Theban, Zethus, Amphion, Orpheus, Musaeus, Socrates, Plato, Aristotle, Aristoxenus, and Timotheus bestowed such labor upon the liberal art of music that, on the testimony of Cicero,[3] they attained a comprehension of almost all its powers and its infinite material, and although for this reason many of the Greeks believed that certain of these men, and especially Pythagoras, had invented the very beginnings of music; nevertheless we know almost nothing of their mode of performing and writing music. Yet it is probable that this was most elegant, for they bestowed on this science, which Plato calls the mightiest of all,[4] their highest learning, so that they taught it to all the ancients, nor was anyone ignorant of music considered an educated man. And how potent, pray, must have been that melody by whose virtue gods, ancestral spirits, unclean demons, animals without reason, and things insensate were said to be moved! This (even if in part fabulous) is not devoid of mystery, for the poets would not have feigned such things of music had they not apprehended its marvelous power with a certain divine vigor of the mind.

But, after the fullness of time, in which the greatest of musicians, Jesus Christ, in whom is our peace, in duple proportion made two natures one, there have flourished in His church many wonderful musicians, as Gregory, Ambrose, Augustine, Hilary, Boethius, Martianus, Guido, and Jean de Muris, of whom some established the usage of singing in the salutary church itself, others composed numerous hymns and canticles for that purpose, others bequeathed to posterity the divinity, others the theory, others the practice of this art, in manuscripts now everywhere dispersed.

Lastly the most Christian princes, of whom, most pious King, you are

---

[2] Genesis 4:21.
[3] De oratore, I, iii, 10.

[4] Republic, 401D (S.R. I, 8).

by far the foremost in the gifts of mind, of body, and of fortune, desiring to augment the divine service, founded chapels after the manner of David, in which at extraordinary expense they appointed singers to sing pleasant and comely praise to our God [5] with diverse (but not adverse) voices. And since the singers of princes, if their masters are endowed with the liberality which makes men illustrious, are rewarded with honor, glory, and wealth, many are kindled with a most fervent zeal for this study.

At this time, consequently, the possibilities of our music have been so marvelously increased that there appears to be a new art, if I may so call it, whose fount and origin is held to be among the English, of whom Dunstable stood forth as chief. Contemporary with him in France were Dufay and Binchoys, to whom directly succeeded the moderns Ockeghem, Busnoys, Regis and Caron, who are the most excellent of all the composers I have ever heard. Nor can the English, who are popularly said to shout while the French sing,[6] stand comparison with them. For the French contrive music in the newest manner for the new times, while the English continue to use one and the same style of composition, which shows a wretched poverty of invention.

But alas! I have perceived that not only these, but many other famous composers whom I admire, while they compose with much subtlety and ingenuity and with incomprehensible sweetness, are either wholly ignorant of musical proportions or indicate incorrectly the few that they know. I do not doubt that this results from a defect in arithmetic, a science without which no one becomes eminent, even in music, for from its innermost parts all proportion is derived.

Therefore, to the purpose that young men who wish to study the liberal and honorable art of music may not fall into similar ignorance and error in proportions, and in praise of God, by whom proportions were given, and for the splendor of your most consecrated Majesty, whose piety surpasses that of all other pious princes, and in honor of your most well-proportioned chapel, whose like I cannot easily believe to exist anywhere in the world, I enter, with the greatest facility my powers permit, upon this work, which with appropriateness to its subject I conclude should be called the Proportional of Music. If I have ventured in it to oppose many, indeed nearly all famous musicians, I entreat that this be by no means ascribed to arrogance. Contending under the banner of truth, I do not order that my writings should neces-

---

5 Psalm 147:1.
6 Cf. Ornithoparcus, *Musice active micrologus*

(Leipzig, 1516), IV, viii, or Pietro Aron, *Lucidario* (Venice, 1545), f. 31.

sarily be followed more than those of others. What in their writings I find correct, I approve; what wrong, I rebuke. If to my readers I seem to carry on this my tradition with justice, I exhort them to put their trust in me; if without justice, let them rather believe others, for I am as ready to be refuted by others as to refute them.

2. Joannes Tinctoris

Liber de arte contrapuncti [1]

[*1477*]

The Book of the Art of Counterpoint, by Master Joannes Tinctoris, Juris-consult, Musician, and Chaplain to His Most Serene Highness the King of Sicily, begins with good omen.

DEDICATION

To THE MOST sacred and glorious prince, Ferdinand, by the Grace of God King of Jerusalem and Sicily, Joannes Tinctoris, the least among his musicians, presents undying reverence.

Long ago, most sagacious King, I found in Horace's *Art of Poetry* this line, remarkable for its elegance and truth:

Understanding is both the first principle and the source of sound writing.[2]

For this reason, before undertaking to write about music, I have sought by listening, reading, and constant practice to obtain as full an under-standing as I could of the various matters that have to do with it.

Though I have heard Wisdom herself cry out: "I love them that love me, and those who keep watch for me will find me,"[3] and have approached my task with steadfast confidence, I confess that as yet I have scarcely swallowed a single drop from her fountain. And this drop, though it be one of the smallest, it is my task to impart to attentive and docile minds through the slender lines traced by my pen, not to deck myself thereby with glory, as Pliny [4] reproached the illustrious author Livy for having done, but to serve posterity, which Cicero [5] declares to

---

1 Text: CS, IV, 76b–77b. The treatise is dated
Naples, October 11, 1477.
2 *Ars poetica,* 309.

3 Proverbs 8:17.
4 *Naturalis historia,* Praefatio, 12.
5 *Tusculan Disputations.* I, 35.

be the task of every excellent man in due proportion to his intellectual power, lest I should hide in the earth the talent given me by God,[6] who in the book of the Prophet is called the Lord of Knowledge,[7] and be cast into outer darkness, where is weeping and gnashing of teeth, as an unprofitable servant of the Lord.[8]

Now therefore, I have decided to set down in full, among other things, what little I have learned, through ever-watchful study, of the art of counterpoint for the benefit of all students of this honorable art, which, of the consonances declared by Boethius to govern all the delectation of music, is contrived for the glory and honor of His eternal majesty to whom, by this very counterpoint, pleasant and comely praise is offered, as commanded in the Psalm.[9]

Before carrying out this project, I cannot pass over in silence the opinion of numerous philosophers, among them Plato and Pythagoras and their successors Cicero, Macrobius, Boethius, and our Isidore, that the spheres of the stars revolve under the guidance of harmonic modulation, that is, by the consonance of various concords. But when, as Boethius relates,[10] some declare that Saturn moves with the deepest sound and that, as we pass by stages through the remaining planets, the moon moves with the highest, while others, conversely, ascribe the deepest sound to the moon and the highest to the sphere of the fixed stars, I put faith in neither opinion. Rather I unshakeably credit Aristotle[11] and his commentator,[12] along with our more recent philosophers, who most manifestly prove that in the heavens there is neither actual nor potential sound. For this reason it will never be possible to persuade me that musical concords, which cannot be produced without sound, can result from the motion of the heavenly bodies.

Concords of sounds and melodies, from whose sweetness, as Lactantius says,[13] the pleasure of the ear is derived, are produced, then, not by heavenly bodies, but by earthly instruments with the co-operation of nature. To these concords the ancient musicians—Plato, Pythagoras, Nicomachus, Aristoxenus, Philolaus, Archytas, Ptolemy, and many others, including even Boethius—most assiduously applied themselves, yet how they were accustomed to arrange and to form them is almost unknown to our generation. And if I may refer to my own experience, I have had in my hands

---

6 Matthew 25:25.
7 I Samuel 2:3.
8 Matthew 25:30.
9 Psalm 147:1.
10 De institutione musica, I, xxvii (Friedlein, p. 219).

11 De caelo, 290B.
12 Thomas Aquinas, In libro Aristotelis de caelo et mundo expositio, II, xiv (Opera, III [Rome, 1886], 173–177).
13 Divinarum institutionum, VI, xxi (Migne, P.L., VI, 713).

certain old songs, called apocrypha, of unknown origin, so ineptly, so stupidly composed that they rather offended than pleased the ear.

Further, although it seems beyond belief, there does not exist a single piece of music, not composed within the last forty years, that is regarded by the learned as worth hearing. Yet at this present time, not to mention innumerable singers of the most beautiful diction, there flourish, whether by the effect of some celestial influence or by the force of assiduous practice, countless composers, among them Jean Ockeghem, Jean Regis, Antoine Busnoys, Firmin Caron, and Guillaume Faugues, who glory in having studied this divine art under John Dunstable, Gilles Binchoys, and Guillaume Dufay, recently deceased. Nearly all the works of these men exhale such sweetness that in my opinion they are to be considered most suitable, not only for men and heroes, but even for the immortal gods. Indeed, I never hear them, I never examine them, without coming away happier and more enlightened. As Virgil took Homer for his model in that divine work the *Aeneid*, so I, by Hercules, have used these composers as models for my modest works, and especially in the arrangement of the concords I have plainly imitated their admirable style of composing.

Finally, most excellent of kings, not unmindful what a rich outpouring of friendliness, by which I mean benevolence, you continue to bestow upon me in accordance with your exceptional humanity, I have undertaken to dedicate this little work to your most distinguished name, hoping that it will serve as dry wood by which the unfailing fire of the charity with which your most illustrious Majesty has heretofore favored me will long burn the more brightly. For it is most manifest that this proceeds from your virtue alone, than which, as Cicero says,[14] nothing is worthier of love.

---

14 *Laelius de amicitia liber*, viii, 28.

3. Bartolomé Ramos

The *Musica practica* of Bartolomé Ramos was printed in Bologna in 1482. Of the life of its author we know almost nothing. That he came from Baeza, near Madrid, and lectured in Bologna, after having previously lectured in Salamanca, is set forth in his book. Other sources tell us that, after leaving Bologna, he went to Rome, where he was still living in 1491.

From his pupil Giovanni Spataro we also learn that Ramos withheld parts of his book from the printer with a view to lecturing on them publicly; as we have it, the *Musica practica* is only a fragment. Those parts that were printed are none the less of extraordinary interest, for in them Ramos advances a novel division of the monochord which results in intervals largely identical with those of just intonation. Although he professes to owe this discovery to his reading of ancient authors, it seems on the whole more probable that he hit upon it empirically. He is himself scarcely aware of the implications of what he is advancing and claims no special virtue for his division beyond its ready intelligibility and the ease with which it can be carried out. Naturally enough, this radical break with tradition aroused a storm of protest. Ramos was violently attacked by Niccolo Burzio in his *Musices opusculum* (1487), just as his pupil Spataro was attacked later on by Franchino Gafori in his *Apologia* (1520). In the end, however, twice defended by Spataro, who replied both to Burzio and to Gafori, modified by Fogliano, and developed by Zarlino, the new teaching won out despite all opposition.

From the Musica practica [1]

[1482]

Part One—First Treatise

2. THE DIVISION OR COMPOSITION OF THE REGULAR MONOCHORD

THE REGULAR monochord has been subtly divided by Boethius [2] with numbers and measure. But although this division is useful and pleasant to theorists, to singers it is laborious and difficult to understand. And since we have promised to satisfy both, we shall give a most easy division of the regular monochord. Let no one think that we have found this with ordinary labor, we who have indeed discovered it reading the precepts of the ancients in many vigils and avoiding the errors of the moderns with care. And anyone even moderately informed will be able to understand it.

Let there be taken a string or chord of any length, and let this be stretched over a piece of wood having a certain concavity, and let the end to which the string is bound be marked at the point *a*. And let the end to which the string is drawn and stretched, placed in a straight line and at a distance, be marked at the point *q*. Now let the quantity *aq*, that is, the length of the whole string, be divided into two equal parts, and let the point of equal distance be marked with the letter *h*. The quantity *ha* we again divide in half, and in the middle of the division we put the letter *d*. The quantity *hd* is again bisected, and in the middle of the section the letter *f* is set down.

Understand the same to be done also with the other half of the string, that is, with *hq*, for in the first division the letter *p* will be inscribed at the midpoint, and in the division *hp* the letter *l* will be put equidistant from either end, and between *l* and *p*, when the same rule of intervals has been observed, we shall introduce the letter *n*. And when we divide *fn* by half we inscribe the letter *i*.

But we shall not go on to smaller parts by means of this division by half until we have made other divisions. Thus we divide the whole,

1 Text: The reprint of the original edition (Bologna, 1482) edited by Johannes Wolf in *Publikationen der Internationalen Musikgesellschaft, Beihefte,* II (Leipzig, 1901), 4–5, 96–99.

2 *De institutione musica,* IV, v.

aq, by three, and measuring from *q*, we put the letter *m* at the end of one third and the letter *e* at the end of two thirds. Then let *eq* be again divided by three, and going from *q* toward *e*, let the sign ♮ quadrum be set down at two thirds and, when the quantity ♮ quadrum to *q* has been doubled, let the letter *b* be inscribed.

Now we again bisect the quantity *mh*, and we mark the middle of the section with the letter *k*. And when we double the quantity *kq*, we put the letter *c* at the end of the duplication. Now between *e* and ♮ quadrum let the letter *g* stand equidistant from either end. Then when we divide *gq* into two equal parts, we inscribe the letter *o*.

Thus the whole monochord has been divided by a legitimate partition, as you will see in the diagram below.[8]

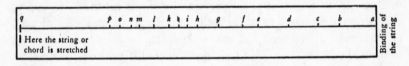

Part Three—Second Treatise

3. IN WHICH THE DIVISIONS OF THE PRIMARY MONOCHORD ARE APPLIED TO NUMERICAL RATIOS

In the first division of our regular monochord we have said that Boethius subtly divided his by numbers and measure. We, however, for the sake of the young, have divided ours by vulgar fractions and with respect to continuous quantity in order that the student may not need first to know both arithmetic and geometry. For to require this would be to fall into the error which we have forbidden ourselves, seeing that we have said that he will need neither of these things to understand our teaching, provided only he be informed in the first rudiments. Thus we have said that a string was to be divided in half, or that a quantity was to be doubled, tripled, or divided by three, expressions most familiar to everyone.

Now, however, seeing that we have determined certain things about discrete quantity, that is, about numbers and numerical proportions, which we know to be most necessary to singers, applying to numerical ratio the same vulgar fractions of the string which we have put forward, we shall show the proportions in which these consist.

---

8 In I, ii, 5, Ramos gives additional directions for finding the lower b-flat and the half-steps e-flat, a-flat, f-sharp, and c-sharp of both octaves. These are of course obtained by proceeding in octaves, fourths, and fifths from *i* and *b*.

Let us assume that the whole length of the string, from *a* to *q*, is 24 inches. Then when we bisect it, marking the section with the letter *h*, *qh* with 12 inches corresponds to *qa* with 24 in duple relationship. Now if you will strike the whole length of the string, and when you have carefully considered the sound, you will put your finger on the point *h* and strike the string *hq*, you will perceive the sounding of the diapason. Thus the diapason is said to be in duple ratio [2:1]. But when we divide *ha* in half, inscribing the letter *d* in the middle, the string *dq* is left with 18 inches, which, compared to the whole, is governed by sesquitertia proportion [4:3]. Thus *d* to *a* is the symphony of the diatessaron. And when we bisect the quantity *hq*, putting the letter *p* in the middle of the section, *pq* is left with only 6 inches, which multiplied by four equals 24. Thus the ratio will necessarily be quadruple [4:1], and *p* to *a* will sound the melody of the double diapason. Then when *hp* has been divided in half and the section inscribed with the letter *l*, we duly perceive the quantity of *lq* to be 9 inches. And if we compare this to the whole we shall find duple superbipartient ratio [8:3], governing the symphony of the diapason plus diatessaron, which, as Boethius says,[4] only Ptolemy admits among the consonances. But we pass over these matters here, both because with the aid of experience we are about to show certain things in composition for three and four voices and because, a little later, with the aid of reason we shall say many things in speculation.

When dividing the whole string by three we put the letters *m* and *e* at one third and two thirds, going from *q* toward *e*, we show clearly that *mq* has 8 inches, which multiplied by three equals 24. Thus, governed by triple proportion [3:1], it sounds to the whole string the symphony of the diapason plus diapente. But *eq* is 16, which is found to be in sesquialtera ratio [3:2] to the whole. Thus it sounds the diapente to *aq*.

We now bisect the quantity *hd*, marking the section with the letter *f*. Seeing that *qd* has been shown to have 18 inches, we know for certain that *qf* has 15, which, compared to *qd*, we find in sesquiquinta ratio [6:5]. For 18 exceeds 15 by 3, which is one fifth-part of the smaller term. But if we compare it to *qh* we find it in sesquiquarta ratio [5:4]. From the latter comparison arises the consonance of the ditone or bitone, from the former the species semiditone or trihemitone, which, as has been shown, is formed from the perfect and imperfect tone.[5]

Now if we compare this same quantity, *qf*, to *qa* we find it in supertripartient quintas ratio [8:5]. For 24 exceeds 15 by three fifth-parts of

---

4 *De institutione musica*, V, ix.

5 In I, i, 3, after pointing out that the semitone is not strictly speaking a semitone at all, Ramos calls it an imperfect tone.

the smaller term. From this comparison arises the sound of the diapente plus semitone or minor sixth or minor hexad. But if we relate *qf* to *ql* we find it in superbipartient tertias proportion [5:3]. For 15 exceeds 9 by 6, which is exactly made up of two parts of nine. And this ratio gives rise to the major sixth or major hexad.[6]

Thus, since the fractions are vulgar and not difficult, we make all our divisions most easy. Guido, however, teaches the division of his monochord by nine steps, seeing that, as we have said, the tone is formed in sesquioctave proportion. But this clearly appears laborious and tedious to those who consider it, for it is more difficult to take an eighth part of any whole than to take a half or a third.[7] And the tone is found effectively by our division, just as it is by his, for example in the interval *d* to *e*, measured by the numbers 18 and 16, or in the interval *l* to *m*, expressed by the ambitus of the numbers 9 and 8.

But enough of these things. Let us now inquire which semitones of the monochord are to be sung and which are, as it seems, to be avoided, since one is found to be larger and the other smaller.[8]

---

6 The reader is advised to work out the entire scale for himself, adopting 288 as the length of the whole string in order that all measurements may be in integers. Without anticipating the results of this operation, it may be said that the scale of Ramos closely approximates the "pure scale" worked out later by Fogliano and Zarlino, and that in the octave F to f (with b-flat) it is actually identical with it. The C octave of Ramos, with its symmetrical construction, is even superior to the "pure scale" from a melodic point of view (cf. Joseph Yasser, *A Theory of Evolving Tonality*, New York, 1932, pp. 215–217).

7 "An eighth part" does not make sense in this context, for Guido, who gives two methods for dividing the monochord (cf. p. 106 above, note 6), divides by two, four, and nine, but not by eight. Perhaps Ramos is thinking of Boethius, who works from the higher pitches toward the lower ones, obtaining the tone (9:8) by adding eighths rather than by subtracting ninths.

8 The major and minor semitones of Ramos have the porportions 16:15 and 135:128.

4. Pietro Aron

Born about 1490 in Florence, Aron (also spelled Aaron) was one of the most important writers on musical theory in the first half of the sixteenth century. Thanks to the influence of a patron he was made a canon of the Cathedral at Rimini. In 1536, however, Aron became a monk of the order of the Bearers of the Cross, first at Bergamo, later at Padua and Venice; he died in 1545.

Aron's published works on musical theory comprise the *Libri III de institutione harmonica* (1516), the *Trattato della natura e cognizione di tutti gli toni di canto figurato* (1525), the *Lucidario in musica* (1545), and the *Compendiolo di molti dubbi* (without date). His chief writing, however, is the *Toscanello in musica* (1523, and four later editions), which contains the best exposition of contrapuntal rules to be found before Zarlino. Aron is the first theorist to recognize the practice of composing all voices of a composition simultaneously.

From the Trattato della natura e cognizione di tutti gli toni di canto figurato [1]

[1525]

I. AN EXPLANATION OF THE FINALS OF ALL THE TONES

JUST AS it is a credit and an honor to any artificer to comprehend and to know and to have a precise understanding of the parts and reasonings of

1 Text: The original edition (Venice, 1525). References to practical examples and certain parentheses of the original are given as author's notes. For a portrait, see Kinsky, p. 109, Fig. 2. As a convenience to the reader, the many examples that Aron cites are listed below in alphabetical order, with indications of the tones to which he assigns them and references to contemporary editions.

6 A l'audience	Heyne	Odhecaton 93
6 Allez regrets	Agricola	Odhecaton 57
5 Alma Redemptoris	Josquin	Corona, III
7 Ascendens Christus	Hylaere	Corona, I
8 Beata Dei Genitrix	Anon	Motetti C
1/2 Beata Dei Genitrix	Mouton	Corona, I
3 Benedic anima mea	Eustachio	Corona, II
6 Brunette	Stokhem	Odhecaton 5

his art, so it is a disgrace and a reproach to him not to know and to be in error among the articles of his faculty. Therefore, when I examined and considered the excellence and grandeur of many, many authors, ancient and modern, there is no manner of doubt that did not assail me inwardly as I reflected on this undertaking, especially since I knew the matter to be most difficult, sublime, and lofty to explain. None the less I intend to relate it to you, most gracious reader, not in a presumptuous or haughty style, but speaking humanely and at your feet. And knowing it to be exacting and strange, I judge that it was abandoned by the celebrated musicians already referred to not through ignorance but merely because it proved otherwise troublesome and exacting at the time. For it is clear that no writers of our age have explained how the many dif-

8 C'est possible	Anon	
2 Ce n'est pas	La Rue	Canti B
– Cela sans plus	Josquin	Odhecaton 61
6 Celeste benefi-cium	Mouton	Corona, I
1/2 Clangat plebs flores	Regis	Motetti a 5
7 Comment peut	Josquin	Canti B
1/2 Congregati sunt	Mouton	Corona, II
2 D'un autre amer	De Orto	Canti B
2 D'un autre amer	Heyne	
2 De tous biens plaine	Heyne	Odhecaton 20
8 Disant adieu madame	Anon	Odhecaton 89
8 E d'en revenez vous	Compère	Canti B
8 E la la la	Anon	Canti B
6 Egregie Christi	Févin	Corona, I
1 Fors seulement	La Rue	Canti B
1 Gaude Barbara	Mouton	Corona, I
1 Gaude Virgo	Festa	
8 Hélas hélas	Ninot	Canti B
1 Hélas qu'il est à mon gré	Japart	Odhecaton 30
5 Hélas que pourra devenir	Caron	Odhecaton 13
– Hélas m'amour	Anon	
5 Illuminare Hie-rusalem	Mouton	Corona, II
3 Interveniat pro rege nostro	Jacotin	Corona, II
8 Je cuide si ce temps	Anon	Odhecaton 2
1 Je dépite tous	Brumel	Canti B
6 Je ne demande	Busnoys	Odhecaton 42
8 Je suis amie	Anon	Canti B
1/2 Judica me Deus	Caen	Corona, II
1 L'homme armé	Josquin	Canti B
8 Ne l'oserai je dire	Anon	Odhecaton 29
– La dicuplaisant	Anon	
1 La plus des plus	Josquin	Odhecaton 64
5 La regretée	Heyne	Canti B
3 Laetatus sum	Eustachio	Corona, II
– Le serviteur	Anon	Odhecaton 35
7 Madame hélas	Josquin	Odhecaton 66
3 Malheur me bat	Ockeghem	Odhecaton 63
7 Mes pensées	Compère	Odhecaton 59
3 Michael archan-gele	Jacotin	Corona, II
3 Miserere	Josquin	Corona, III
1 Missa Ave maris stella	Josquin	Missarum, II
1 Missa D'un autre amer	Josquin	Missarum, II
– Missa de Beata Virgine	Josquin	Missarum, III
5, 7 Missa de Beata Virgine	La Rue	Missae
2 Missa Hercules dux Ferrariae	Josquin	Missarum, II
7 Missa Ut sol	Mouton	
7 Mittit ad Vir-ginem	Anon	Motetti C
8 Mon mari m'a diffamée	De Orto	Canti B
7 Multi sunt vocati	Zanetto	
8 Myn morgem ghaf	Anon	Canti B
1 Nobilis progenie	Févin	Corona, I
1 Nomine qui Domini	Caen	Corona, II
3 Nunca fué pena mayor	Anon	Odhecaton 4
6 O admirabile commercium	Josquin	Antico, I
4 O Maria roga-mus te	Anon	Motetti C
8 O Venus bant	Josquin	Odhecaton 78
– Peccata mea Domine	Mouton	Corona, II
1 Pourquoi fut fuie cette emprise	Anon	Canti B
1 Pourtant si mon	Busnoys	
5 Quaeramus cum pastoribus	Mouton	Antico, I
1/2 Rogamus te Virgo Maria	Jacotin	Corona, II
6 Sancta Trinitas	Févin	Corona, I
8 Si dedero	Agricola	Odhecaton 56
2 Si mieux	Compère	Odhecaton 51
5 Si sumpsero	Obrecht	Canti B
5 Stabat Mater	Josquin	Corona, III
6 Tempus meum	Févin	Corona, I
2 Virgo caelesti	Compère	Canti B
6 Vôtre bargero-nette	Compère	Odhecaton 41
1 Vulnerasti cor meum	Févin	Corona, I

ferent modes are to be recognized, although to their greater credit they have treated of matters which can be readily understood. I, therefore, not moved by ambition of any kind, but as a humble man, have undertaken this task, hoping that in humanity and kindliness my readers will all excuse whatever errors I may make. I show briefly what I know to be necessary, for I see that many are deceived about the true understanding, and regarding this I hope in some measure to satisfy them.

First I intend to explain what is meant by "final" and what by "species" and whether the final is always necessary and rational for the recognition of the tone or whether the tones are sometimes to be recognized from their species. Then I shall show what part the singer ought to examine and how the composer ought to proceed in his composition in accordance with his intention, touching also on certain other secrets which will surely afford you no little delight.

I say, then, that the final being diverse, that is, regular or irregular, it follows that each tone has a similarly diverse form.

From this it follows that at one time the final governs and at another time the species.

"Final" I define in this way: a final is simply a magisterial ending in music, introduced in order that the tone may be recognized. Musicians conclude such an ending regularly or irregularly in order that the nature and form of each tone may be the better understood. Thus the positions D *sol re*, E *la mi*, F *fa ut*, and G *sol re ut* have been constituted regular finals or ending steps for the first and second, third and fourth, fifth and sixth, and seventh and eighth tones, while the steps Gamma *ut*, A *re*, ♮ *mi*, C *fa ut*, A *la mi re*, B *fa* ♮ *mi*, and C *sol fa ut* are called irregular.

In accordance with this understanding, the final remains necessary, rational, and governing to every tone on the above-named regular steps.

The species, then, will govern sometimes regularly and sometimes irregularly.

"Species" is simply the arrangement of the sounds of the genus, varied in definite prescribed ways, as shown in the example.

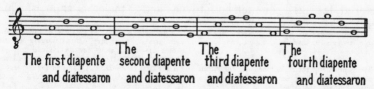

The first diapente   The second diapente   The third diapente   The fourth diapente
and diatessaron   and diatessaron   and diatessaron   and diatessaron

It follows, then, that the final is also necessary in the above-named irregular positions, namely A *la mi re*, B *fa* ♮ *mi*, and C *sol fa ut*. Here we shall consider it in two ways: first, with respect to confinality; second, with respect to the differences of the Saeculorum.[2] Thus, if a composition [a] ends in the position called A *la mi re* and there is no flat in the signature, the final will be common to the first and second tones with respect to confinality and also to the third with respect to difference,[3] provided—as you will understand from what follows—that the procedure in the composition be suited and appropriate to confinality or difference.[4] But if the composition has a flat in the signature, the final will be in my opinion neither necessary nor rational with respect to confinality, for it is clear that the form will differ from its previous state. For this reason, such compositions are to be judged by their species. The same will obviously apply to compositions ending on B *fa* ♮ *mi*, C *sol fa ut*, and all other steps on which the species may occur.

Therefore, the cognition derived from species is necessary understanding and not arbitrary to music. First, because this cognition is by definition true and necessary. Besides this, understanding that is necessary has something essential about it; but the cognition of species is essential and therefore necessary. Besides this, that which demands necessary cognition is *per se;* but the cognition of species is cognition *per se* and therefore necessary. Nor is it an objection that we are for the most part accustomed to base our cognition of music on the final, for I reply that this has been for the sake of readier understanding, inasmuch as those things that are at the end are customarily more closely observed than those that are at the beginning and in the middle.

And that our conclusion is true, we may demonstrate with these and other similar arguments. We say that man is defined as an animal rational and mortal; it is certain that rational and mortal are two differences for knowing what man is; of these, one is final and considered according to the end of man, namely mortal—the other is formal and considered according to the specific and formal being of living man, namely rational; the latter makes the essence of man better known than the former, which considers him according to his end, namely that man is mortal, for this is common both to man and to the other animals. Thus

---

a I speak always of masses, motets, canzoni, frottole, strambotti, madrigali, sonetti, and capitoli.

2 The confinals of the eight tones are, for Aron, the pitches a fifth above (or a fourth below) the established finals. He seems not to have thought it necessary to list the differences.

3 This step is also a difference in the fifth tone (see p. 26).

4 As Aron explains in Chapter 8, suitable and appropriate "procedure" turns largely on the choice of proper steps for medial cadences. In Chapters 9 to 12 these are said to be as follows: for the first tone—D, F, G, and a; for the second —A, C, D, F, G, and a; for the third—E, F, G, a, ♮, and c; for the fourth—C, D, E, F, G, and a; for the fifth—F, a, and c; for the sixth— C, D, F, a, and c; for the seventh—G, a, ♮, c, and d; for the eighth—D, F, G, and c.

the cognition of the end is not cognition *per se* and therefore not always necessary.

And this is demonstrated by certain compositions which, having the ordinary and regular final, but lacking the ascent and descent of some of its species, are not said to be of any tone but (as was shown in Chapter 30 of the first book of another work of mine, *De institutione harmonica*) are merely called *Canti euphoniaci*.

2. HOW THE SINGER OUGHT TO JUDGE THE TONE

The tenor being the firm and stable part, the part, that is, that holds and comprehends the whole concentus of the harmony, the singer must judge the tone by means of this part only. For we see that when a tenor and its cantus are far apart it causes, not pleasure, but little sweetness to those who hear it, something which arises from the distance that lies between the cantus and the contrabassus. The tenor being for this reason better suited to the natural progressions and more easily handled, every composition [b] is in my opinion to be judged by its tenor. For in the tenor the natural form is more readily considered than in the soprano, where, should you wish to form the seventh tone, you would need to find its diatessaron through the accidental course.[5] Thus we prescribe this manner and order for all compositions written at the composer's pleasure, whether upon a plainsong or without regard for one, also for compositions for five, six, seven, and more voices, in which it is usual to write a first and principal tenor. Each of the added parts will be governed by the nature of the tenor, and by means of the tenor the tone will be recognized unless the plainsong itself, which is primary and principal to such a recognition, be in some other part.[6]

---

b Whether Introit, Kyrie, Gloria, Gradual, Alleluia, Credo, Offertory, Sanctus, Agnus Dei, Postcommunion, Respond, Deo gratias, Psalm, Hymn, Magnificat, motet, canzone, frottola, bergerette, strambotto, madrigal, or capitolo.

5 We see, in other words, that when a tenor and its cantus belong to the same tone—and unless this is the case, the cantus can have no bearing on the tonality of the composition—they will lie far apart and the resulting texture will be disagreeable, particularly in view of the disparity between the cantus and the contrabassus. Thus the usual thing will be to make the tenor authentic and the cantus plagal, or vice versa, leaving the tenor as the sole determining factor. Aside from this, "in view of the inconvenience of the upward range," the cantus will seldom

ascend to the octave above the final in the seventh tone or (see p. 25 below) in the transposed third.

6 Cf. Jean Tinctoris, *Liber de natura et proprietate tonorum*, xxiv (CS, IV, 29a–29b): "When some mass or chanson or any other composition you please is made up of various parts, belonging to different tones, if you ask without qualification to what tone such a composition belongs, the person asked ought to reply without qualification according to the quality of the tenor, for in every composition this is the principal part and the basis of the whole relationship. But if it be asked specifically to what tone some single part of such a composition belongs, the person asked will reply specifically, 'To such and such a tone.'"

3. WAYS OF RECOGNIZING THE TONE OF DIFFERENT COMPOSITIONS

Reflecting alone for days and days, I recalled certain projects often in my mind. Wherefore, gracious reader, had not your gentle aspect and my eager wish for the desired end constrained me, I should more lightly have lowered the sails at the hard-won port. But since I think that you by no means blamed it, I wish to pursue the enterprise begun, not for those who turn a thing over and over, but solely for those familiar with this fare. Thus, having reached this point, I am left somewhat in doubt. Yet I intend rather to go on reasoning with you, seeking a rule by means of which you may arrive at a clear understanding of each of the tones in question.

In so far as compositions end in the positions D *sol re*, E *la mi*, F *fa ut*, and G *sol re ut*, they are to be judged according to their finals, and by means of these their true and proper species [c] will be recognized. These are the steps called regular to the first, second, third, fourth, fifth, sixth, seventh, and eighth tones, and on these steps the final will be necessary, rational, and governing.

Let me explain this to you more fully. First consider those compositions that have their final on D *sol re* and that at the beginning or in their course proceed with the species of the third, fourth, fifth, sixth, seventh, or eighth tone; all these are in my opinion to be judged only from their proper and regular final, provided that they contain contradictory and unsuitable procedures, for no other tone has a difference ending on this step. And as to those ending on E *la mi*, these are in my opinion subject in the same way only to their own form. Such compositions are best said to belong to mixed tones (*toni commisti*).[7]

But those compositions that end in the position called F *fa ut* are in my opinion subject not only to their own final and species but also to the nature and form of the first and fourth tones, in view of the difference which these tones sometimes exhibit on this step. Understand, however, that this is when they proceed in the way suited to the first and fourth tones, for otherwise they will remain of the fifth or sixth. Certain others end on G *sol re ut*; these are in my opinion subject to the

---

c Namely, from D *sol re* to the first A *la mi re* and from thence to D *la sol re*, from E *la mi* to B *fa* ♮ *mi* and from thence to high E *la mi*, from F *fa ut* to C *sol fa ut* and from thence to high F *fa ut*, and from low G *sol re ut* to D *la sol re* and from thence to the second G *sol re ut*.

7 Cf. Jean Tinctoris, *Diffinitorium musicae*, xviii (CS, IV, 190b): "A *tonus commixtus* is one which, if authentic, is mixed with a tone other than its plagal, if plagal, with a tone other than its authentic."

seventh and eighth tones and also to the first, second, third, and fourth, as you will understand from what follows.[8]

Certain other compositions end on the irregular steps A *la mi re*, B *fa ♮ mi*, and C *sol fa ut;* these we shall consider according to their procedure, their species, and the differences of the Saeculorum, for these considerations will govern them and yield the true recognition of the tone.

Certain other compositions end on D *la sol re*, E *la mi*, F *fa ut*, and G *sol re ut;* these steps are of the same nature as the regular steps previously named.

Certain other compositions, although they end regularly, have a flat signature; these are to be judged according to their species (excepting those ending on D *sol re*, F *fa ut*, etc.), for the final will now be neither necessary nor rational to the recognition of the tone.

Certain other compositions proceed at the beginning and in their course with the species suited to a given tone but end with species that contradict it; these are to be judged according to the species and differences previously mentioned, excepting (as was noted above) those ending on the regular finals.

Certain other compositions end irregularly and proceed inharmoniously without any complete diapente by means of which their true form might be recognized; these are to be judged by means of some species of diatessaron or by their own finals.

One will also find compositions arbitrarily written without regard to form or regular manner, comparable indeed to players of the game called *alleta,* who agree upon a certain goal at which they will take refuge and, chasing one after another, run back to that place or goal and are safe; of the composers of such works as these we say that they turn aimlessly round and round, progressing and digressing beyond the nature and the primary order that they have in mind until, by some trick, they arrive at an end of their own. Such harmonies or compositions can in my opinion be judged only by means of the final, and then only when they end without a flat signature.

In certain other compositions this signature appears only in the contrabassus, in others only in the tenor; such an arrangement is in our opinion neither permissible nor suitable in a harmony or composition unless it is used deliberately and introduced with art.[d]

---

8 Aron does not refer again to the possibility of endings on F in the first and fourth tones or on G (as difference) in the first, second, and fourth; for the ending on G in the third, see pp. 24–25 below.

d As by the excellent Josquin in the Patrem of his Mass of Our Lady and in a similar way by the divine Alexander [Agricola] in many of his compositions. [As published in Heft 42 of *Das Chorwerk*, the Credo of Josquin's *Missa de Beata*

Certain other compositions have a flat signature on low E *la mi*, the first A *la mi re*, B *fa* ♮ *mi*, and high E *la mi;* whether they end regularly or irregularly, these are in my opinion to be judged according to the species, not according to the final.[e]

4. AN EXPLANATION OF THE FIRST AND SECOND TONES

Every composition in which the tenor ends on D *sol re* is unhesitatingly to be assigned to the first or second tone, the more readily if the soprano end on D *la sol re* with the regular and rational final, clearly showing the natural form.[f] The same is also true of certain other compositions with a flat signature; the nature of these remains unchanged, in my opinion, for only the diatessaron, formed by the interval A *la mi re* to D *la sol re,* is altered. Seeing then that the diapente primary and natural to the tone is left intact, such compositions are also to be assigned to the first tone.[g]

And if sometimes, as has become the custom, the composer prolongs his work, amusing himself with additional progressions, you will, in my opinion, need to consider whether the final, as altered by the composer, is suited to and in keeping or out of keeping with his composition, for if reason guide him in what is suited to the tone he will at least see to it that some one part (namely, the tenor or cantus) sustains the final, while the others proceed as required by the tone, regular or irregular, with pleasing and appropriate progressions like those shown below, or in some more varied manner according to his pleasure and disposition.

Virgine has no signatures whatever. But it is clear from Aron's comment and from the composition itself that the Tenor secundus, following the Tenor in canon at the fifth below, should have the signature one flat.—Ed.]

e For example, "Cela sans plus" by Josquin, "Peccata mea Domine" by Jean Mouton (in the *Motetti della corona*), "Le serviteur," "Hélas m'amour," "La dicuplaisant," &c. [Cf. Jean Tinctoris, *Liber de natura et proprietate tonorum,* xxiv (CS, IV, 29b): "If some one were to say to me, speaking in general, 'Tinctoris, I ask you to what tone the chanson *Le serviteur* belongs,' I would reply, 'Generally speaking, to the first

tone irregular,' since the tenor, or principal part, of this chanson belongs to this tone. But if he were to ask specifically to what tone the superius or contratenor belongs, I would reply specifically that the one and the other belong to the second tone irregular. But there is no one who doubts that a specific question about the tenor is to be answered as was the general one."—Ed.]

f As in the motets "Rogamus te virgo Maria" by Jacotin, "Judica me Deus" by A. Caen, "Congregati sunt" and "Beata Dei genitrix" by Jean Mouton, and "Clangat plebs flores" by Regis.

g As in the motet "Nomine qui Domini" by A. Caen, "Pourquoi fut fuie cette emprise," &c.

But since some will say, perhaps, that the position D *sol re* is common also to the second tone, I shall tell you that in figured music you will very seldom find a tenor with the procedure and downward range suited and appropriate to the second tone as ended in this way. Nevertheless, a composer may wish to proceed in accordance with the nature of the second tone; he will then take care to proceed at the beginning and in the course of his composition with some regard for its proper form, as observed and comprehended in the psalms and the Magnificat, where he is restricted and subject to the manner and order proper to the second tone.

Certain other compositions end on the step G *sol re ut;* with a flat signature, these are in my opinion only to be understood as of the first or second tone, even though this is the step ordinary and regular to the seventh and eighth. For this signature (or figure) alters the form or structure proper and natural to the seventh and eighth tones; at the same time, having acquired the species belonging to the first and second, the final becomes inactive and on this step is left arbitrary and as it were regular *per se,* not suited to the seventh and eighth tones, but necessary to the first and second.[h]

Certain other compositions, ending on this same step, are said to be of the second tone; these are readily recognized by their extended downward range.[i] And if this consideration seem to you not always to the purpose, do not be surprised, for composers sometimes observe the procedure of a given tone at the beginning and in the course of a composition, ending then in accordance with the difference of the plainsong, as you will understand from what follows.

Certain other tenors end on A *la mi re;* here you will need to consider and examine whether their procedure is suited and rational to such an ending, for if a tenor end irregularly in the first or second tone, not proceeding with its proper form, it may easily not belong to it, even though this step is one of its irregular finals and an ending of its Saeculorum or difference. As you will understand from what follows, this is because the third and fourth tones also use this step as a difference. For this reason, then, you will assign such a tenor to the first or second tone only when you find the proper form.[j]

---

h This is demonstrated by the following masses and motets, which are of the first tone in view of their procedure, structure, and complete diapason: *Ave maris stella* and *D'un autre amer* by Josquin, "Nobilis progenie" and "Vulnerasti cor meum" by Févin, &c.

i For example, "Virgo caelesti" by Loyset Compère, "D'un autre amer" and "De tous biens pleine" by Heyne, "Ce n'est pas" by Pierre de La Rue, and "D'un autre amer" by de Orto.

j As in "La plus de plus" by Josquin, which is of the first tone in view of the course of its diapente and its upward range, or in "Si mieux" by Loyset Compère, which is of the second, as will be readily evident.

Certain other compositions end on D *la sol re;* these are in my opinion to be assigned in the same way to the first and second tones, for it is clearly evident that from D *la sol re* to its diapason is the proper form of the first diapente and diatessaron, namely *re-la* and *re-sol.* When they ascend as far as the fifth or sixth step, and especially when they ascend still further, they will be of the first tone.[k] But when they lack this extension to the upper limit of the diapente, proceeding rather in the lower register, they will be of the second tone and not of the first.[l] This opinion of mine is supported by the venerable Father Zanetto, a musician of Venice.

5. AN EXPLANATION OF THE THIRD AND FOURTH TONES

The few who fish in these waters are in the habit of saying that every composition ending in the position E *la mi* is to be assigned to the fourth tone. They forget that this step is common also to the third, and in so doing seem to me to involve themselves in no little difficulty. Seeing that the difference often ends on this step in the fourth tone, many, thinking only of the ending of its Saeculorum, judge a composition to belong to it. Thus the greatest confusion may easily arise. It is accordingly necessary to consider at various times the final, the upward and downward range, the procedures, the intonations, and the differences, which, since they are of different sorts, end naturally in different ways.[m]

Certain other compositions ending in the position G *sol re ut* are said to be of the third tone, even though this is the step ordinary and regular to the seventh and eighth. You will need to give your most careful consideration to these and, above all, to their procedure, for unless they have the form and order due and appropriate to the third

---

k Whether with a flat signature, as in "Pourtant si mon" by Antoine Busnoys, "Gaude virgo" a motet by Costanzo Festa, "L'homme armé" *et sic de singulis* by Josquin, and "Hélas qu'il est à mon gré" by Japart; or without, as in "Fors seulement" by Pierre de La Rue, "Je dépite tous" by Brumel, and "Gaude Barbara" by Jean Mouton.

l For example, the mass *Hercules dux Ferrariae,* composed by Josquin, and many other works which I shall not enumerate, since you will readily understand them from their similarity to this one.

m Thus, in the motet "Michael archangele" by Jacotin, the first part is in my opinion of the irregular third tone while the second ends in the regular third tone, not in the fourth; the same is true of "Malheur me bat" by Ockeghem, "Interveniat pro rege nostro" by Jacotin, and many other compositions, similar to these and having the regular final and the required procedure and upward range.

tone, with this final they will never be assigned to it, but rather to the seventh or eighth. But where the natural form is found, they will always be assigned to the third tone, and not to the seventh or eighth, in view of their form and difference.[n] This opinion is likewise supported by the venerable Father Zanetto, Venetian musician.

You will also find certain other compositions ending on A *la mi re;* when these observe the appropriate procedure they will be assigned to the third tone.[o] But when they have a flat signature, they are in my opinion to be assigned to the third tone the more readily, even though at the beginning and in their course they fail to proceed in the due and appropriate way, for it is evident that the regular structure of the tone [p] will prevail. But because of the inconvenience of their upward range, few such pieces will be found, unless written for equal voices or *voci mutate.* Compositions of this sort are to be assigned to the third or fourth tone in view of their species and downward range, not because of their difference or procedure. Thus it may be inferred that, in view of their extended downward range, they will in preference be assigned to the fourth tone.[q]

6. AN EXPLANATION OF THE FIFTH AND SIXTH TONES

Spurred on by your affection and with my goal in sight, I turn to the question about which you may have been in doubt.[9] Thus, in beginning this part of my explanation, I ask you to observe that compositions ending in the position F *fa ut* are to be assigned to the fifth or sixth tone. On this point I should like to remove any remaining uncertainty, for seeing that such compositions very often—indeed, almost always—have the flat signature and that the form of the tone is altered, it would be easy for you to believe the contrary, in view of certain opinions that I have expressed above. Know, then, that in compositions such as these the older composers were more concerned with facility than with proper form and correct structure. For the fifth and sixth tones often require the help of the b-flat, although always to use it would be contrary to the tendencies of the mediations of these tones as laid down by the ancients. This opinion is likewise supported by the

---

n For example, "Nunca fué pena mayor," &c.

o For example, "Miserere mei Deus" by Josquin, "Laetatus sum" by Eustachio, "Benedic anima mea Dominum," in which the first part ends on the confinal, the second on the final, and the third on the difference, &c.

p Namely, *mi-mi* and *mi-la*, arising from the interval A *la mi re* to high E *la mi,* to which is added the upper diatessaron *mi-la.*

q For example, "O Maria rogamus te" in the

Motetti C and many others which you will readily recognize on the same principle.

9 The reader, that is, having been told that in the D and F modes the flat signature does not effect a transposition (p. 21), and having seen that the explanation of this given for the D modes (p. 22) will not apply to the F, will have anticipated a difficulty at this point.

previously mentioned Venetian, Father Zanetto. For this reason, then, the older composers altered the third diapente, giving it the nature of the fourth, in order that the tritone which would otherwise occur in running through it might not cause inconvenience or harshness in their music.[r]

And if certain other compositions, ending on A *la mi re,* are to be assigned to the fifth tone, know that at the beginning and in their course these must observe a procedure suited to it; lacking this, the difference will have little force and, as previously explained, they may easily be of some other tone. Nevertheless, the composer may if he pleases observe this tone, but what is necessary will be recognized more clearly in the psalms and the Magnificat. The sixth tone we do not concede on this step, for it has neither the form nor the difference.

Certain other compositions ending on B *fa ♮ mi* are said to be of the fifth tone, but we do not approve this in the absence of the flat signature (or figure) which on this step produces the proper structure both ascending and descending. Here, then, the final is rational, necessary, and governing, and in this way the proper form is recognized.[s]

Certain other compositions, ending on C *sol fa ut,* are said to be of the fifth tone, both with and without the flat signature;[t] this is solely in view of the difference which the plainsong sometimes exhibits here. The sixth tone is lacking on this step, even though it is the confinal of the fifth and sixth tones regularly ended, for the step can bear no form or difference appropriate to it.

---

[r] This is uniformly demonstrated in the following compositions of the fifth tone, compositions which cannot be otherwise assigned in view of their upward range and procedure: "Stabat mater dolorosa" and "Alma Redemptoris" by Josquin, "Hélas que pourra devenir" by Caron, "Quaeramus cum pastoribus" and "Illuminare illuminare Jerusalem" by Jean Mouton, and the Sanctus and Agnus Dei of the Mass of Our Lady by Pierre de La Rue. Those which do not have this extended upward range, falling short of the diapente or hexachord, are to be assigned to the sixth tone as regularly ended, for example, "Brunette" by Stokhem. "Vôtre bergeronette" by

Compère, "Je ne demande" by Busnoys, "Allez regrets" by Agricola, "A l'audience" by Heyne, "Sancta Trinitas unus Deus" and "Tempus meum est ut revertar ad eum" by Févin, "Celeste beneficium" by Jean Mouton, "Egregie Christi" by Févin, &c.

[s] As demonstrated in the chanson "La regretée," composed by Heyne, which is of the fifth tone in view of its species, cadences, and upward range; or in "O admirabile commercium" by Josquin, which is said to be of the sixth, as are certain others similar to it, although there are few of these.

[t] For example, "Si sumpsero" by Obrecht.

7. AN EXPLANATION OF THE SEVENTH AND EIGHTH TONES

Certain persons have held that the seventh and eighth tones may end regularly and irregularly on three steps, namely Gamma *ut*, C *fa ut*, and G *sol re ut*, and regarding these endings many advance many different opinions, especially regarding those on Gamma *ut* and C *fa ut*. Compositions ending on these steps they assign rather to the seventh tone than to the eighth, and this because such a composition seldom if ever descends as the plagal form requires. In view of this confusion I shall tell you that I cannot admit such opinions, for it is clear that these compositions continue to observe the natural requirements of the proper and regular tones. Those ending on Gamma *ut*, in view of their acquired form, peculiar to the seventh tone, I take to be of this tone and not of the eighth when they are without the flat signature, but of the first or second when they have it. But those ending on C *fa ut*, for the reason given above and also because they do not have the proper diatessaron, I assign to the eighth tone and not to the seventh.[u] This opinion is likewise held by the previously mentioned musician, Father Zanetto.

Certain other compositions end in the position G *sol re ut;* these are naturally and regularly to be assigned to the seventh tone or to the eighth in view of their proper final and natural form.[v]

Certain other compositions end in the position C *sol fa ut;* these are in my opinion to be assigned in the same way to the seventh tone or to the eighth in view of their difference and procedure, the difference often ending on this step. Thus, if such a composition proceed in the appropriate way it will most certainly be of the seventh tone or of the eighth in view of its final, still more reasonably so if it has the flat signa-

u As demonstrated in the following compositions: "Mon mari m'a diffamée" by de Orto and the chanson called "E la la la"; following the same principle you will understand the rest.

v Thus the mass *Ut sol* by Jean Mouton and the Gloria of Our Lady by Pierre de La Rue are in our opinion to be assigned to the seventh tone in view of their species, their final, and their extended upward range; the same applies to "Multi sunt vocati pauci vero electi" by the venerable Father Zanetto of Venice and "Ascen-

dens Christus in altum" by Hylaere. But "Si dedero" by Alexander Agricola and "C'est possible que l'homme peut" will be of the eighth tone in view of their final and their procedure; the same is true of "O Venus bant" by Josquin, "Disant adieu madame," "Je suis amie," "Min morghem ghaf," "Hélas hélas" by Ninot, "E d'en revenez vous" by Compère, "Beata Dei genitrix," and many others which you will recognize on the same principle.

ture, for this will give it the proper structure, namely *ut-sol* and *re-sol*, the form peculiar to the seventh and eighth tones.[w]

Following these principles in your examinations and reflecting on the method set forth above, you will have a clear understanding of any other composition or tone suited and appropriate to figured music.

---

[w] Thus "Mes pensées" by Compère, "Madame hélas" and "Comment peut" by Josquin, and "Mittit ad virginem" can be assigned only to the seventh tone. But "Je cuide si ce temps" and "Ne l'oserai je dire" will be of the eighth tone and not of the seventh, as their form and extended downward procedure will show you.

5. Heinrich Glarean

Born in the Canton of Glarus in Switzerland in 1488, Glarean died in 1563 in Freiburg. Known as Glareanus, he was one of the great humanists of the sixteenth century. A friend of Erasmus of Rotterdam, he was a philosopher, theologian, philologist, historian, poet, and musical scholar, crowned poet laureate by Emperor Maximilian I. Among his works of interest to the musical reader, the most important is the *Dodecachordon* (i.e., the "instrument of twelve-strings"), which advocated four additions to the existing eight ecclesiastical modes. The book had a tremendous influence on the changing concept of the modal system. Glareanus also revised the works of Boethius, the edition being posthumously published by M. Rota in 1570. The *Dodecachordon* interests the historian not only because of its discussion of the ever-present problem of the modes but also because it contains many illuminating examples illustrating the intricate contrapuntal art of the time.

From the Dodecachordon

[1547]

Book Three—Chapter 24

Examples of the Paired Combinations of the Modes
together with
An Encomium of Josquin Desprez [1]

So MUCH for our examples of the twelve modes in that varied sort of music not (at least in our opinion) inappropriately called mensural, ex-

---

1 Text: The original edition (Basle, 1547). The musical examples are omitted. For the title page in facsimile, see Kinsky, p. 58, Fig. 3. German translation by Peter Bohn (with the musical examples in score) in *Publikationen älterer praktischer und theoretischer Musikwerke*, xvi (Leipzig, 1888).

amples cited with all possible brevity from various authors in proof
of those things that have seemed to us in need of proof. It now remains for us to give examples of these same modes in combination,[2]
not commonplace examples, to be sure, but weighty ones elegantly illustrating the matter. And since in our preceding book [3] we have sufficiently discussed the actual nature of these combinations, we shall refrain from re-examining it here. All our examples will be in the order
seen in our last book; thus, having begun with Dorian and Hypodorian,
we shall then add examples of the other paired combinations, briefly expressing our opinion about these, partly to show others a better way
of judging and, as it were, to open men's eyes, partly to make known
the merits of the ingenious in this art, merits which to certain sufficiently
hostile judges seem commonplace, but which to us seem considerable
and most worthy of admiration.

Now in this class of authors and in this great crowd of the ingenious
there stands out as by far pre-eminent in temperament, conscientious-
ness, and industry (or I am mistaken in my feeling) Jodocus à Prato,
whom people playfully (ὑποκοριστικῶς) call in his Belgian mother-
tongue Josquin, as though they were to say "Little Jodocus." If this
man, besides that native bent and strength of character by which he was
distinguished, had had an understanding of the twelve modes and of
the truth of musical theory, nature could have brought forth nothing
more majestic and magnificent in this art; so versatile was his temperament in every respect, so armed with natural acumen and force, that there
is nothing he could not have done in this profession. But moderation
was wanting for the most part and, with learning, judgment; thus in
certain places in his compositions he did not, as he should have, soberly
repress the violent impulses of his unbridled temperament. Yet let this
petty fault be condoned in view of the man's other incomparable gifts.

No one has more effectively expressed the passions of the soul in music
than this symphonist, no one has more felicitously begun, no one has
been able to compete in grace and facility on an equal footing with him,
just as there is no Latin poet superior in the epic to Maro. For just as
Maro, with his natural facility, was accustomed to adapt his poem to his
subject so as to set weighty matters before the eyes of his readers with
close-packed spondees, fleeting ones with unmixed dactyls, to use words

---

2 Examples, that is, in which the tenor, or principal part, has the combined plagal and authentic
range.

3 II, xxviii–xxxv, pp. 138–161 (Bohn's translation, pp. 105–119).

suited to his every subject, in short, to undertake nothing inappropriately, as Flaccus says of Homer, so our Josquin, where his matter requires it, now advances with impetuous and precipitate notes, now intones his subject in long-drawn tones, and, to sum up, has brought forth nothing that was not delightful to the ear and approved as ingenious by the learned, nothing, in short, that was not acceptable and pleasing, even when it seemed less erudite, to those who listened to it with judgment. In most of his works he is the magnificent virtuoso, as in the *Missa super voces musicales* [4] and the *Missa ad fugam;* [5] in some he is the mocker, as in the *Missa La sol fa re mi;* [6] in some he extends himself in rivalry,[7] as in the *Missa de Beata Virgine;* [8] although others have also frequently attempted all these things, they have not with the same felicity met with a corresponding success in their undertakings.

This was for us the reason why in this, the consummation of our work, we have by preference cited examples by this man. And although his talent is beyond description, more easily admired than properly explained, he still seems preferable to others, not only for his talent, but also for his diligence in emending his works. For those who have known him say that he brought his things forth with much hesitation and with corrections of all sorts, and that he gave no composition to the public unless he had kept it by him for several years, the opposite of what we said Jacob Obrecht is reported to have done. Hence some not inappropriately maintain that the one may justly be compared to Virgil, the other to Ovid. But if we admit this, to whom shall we more fittingly compare Pierre de La Rue, an astonishingly delightful composer, than to Horace, Isaac than perhaps to Lucan, Févin than to Claudianus, Brumel to Statius? Yet I should seem foolish, and rightly, if I were to speak with so little taste of these men, and perhaps I should deserve to hear that popular saying, "Shoemaker, stick to your last!" Hence I proceed to the explanation and judging of the examples.

Of the first combination, that of Dorian and Hypodorian, let our example be the melody "Victimae paschali laudes," on the Blessed Resurrection of Christ, as set by this same author Josquin,[9] a melody that we

---

4 *Werken, Missen,* I (Amsterdam, 1926), 1–32.

5 *Missarum Josquin Liber III* (Venice, 1514). For a brief account of this work, see A. W. Ambros, *Geschichte der Musik,* III (3d ed., Leipzig, 1893), 220–221; the "Pleni sunt coeli" is given by Glarean (III, xiii, p. 258; Bohn's translation, pp. 204–205).

6 *Werken, Missen,* I (Amsterdam, 1926), 35–56.

7 With Antoine Brumel (see p. 35).

8 Das Chorwerk, VIII (Wolfenbüttel, 1936), Heft 42.

9 Glarean gives the complete musical text of the seven examples discussed in this chapter, and all of them are printed in score in Bohn's translation. We add, wherever possible, references to more recent and more readily accessible editions, in this instance to Josquin Desprez, *Werken, Motetten,* I (Amsterdam, 1926), 136–139.

have mentioned twice before and that we have further cited as an example of this combination in our second book.[10] In it, it will rightly be judged ingenious that the given theme is heard thus divided by intervals among the four voices, as is most fitting.[11] In its first part, the highest voice, borrowed from some well-known song,[12] presents the Hypodorian mode with an added ditone below. In the following part it is Dorian with an added diatessaron above. Here the ending is on the highest step of the diapason, whereas just the other way it ought to have been on the lowest; this part, however, is also borrowed,[13] and on this account he has not wished to alter it. The tenor is extended a ditone lower than the Hypodorian form requires, but the author does this with his usual license. The borrowed melodies he combines with other ancient ones, appropriately in the same mode, for melodies in other modes would not agree to this extent. At the same time, it was not difficult for this author to combine melodies belonging to different modes, even to do so gracefully, for he composed scarcely a single mass, be its mode what it may, without bringing in the Aeolian mode in the Nicene Creed,[14] something that others have attempted also, but not always with the same success. Each voice has something worthy of note, thus the tenor its stability, the bass its wonderful gravity, although I scarcely know whether it pleases everyone that he ascends as he does in the bass at the word "Galilaea." That this proceeds from the wantonness of his temperament we cannot deny; thus we must accept it gracefully as an addition. The cantus has an ancient flavor; the seventh note from the end is heard alone, with all the other voices pausing. Yet, in comparison with the genius of the man, all these things are wholly unimportant. Let us go on, then, to other examples.

Here, in the motet "De profundis," [15] I wish everyone to observe closely what the beginning is like and with how much passion and how much majesty the composer has given us the opening words; instead of transposing the modes from their natural positions to the higher register (as is elsewhere the usual custom), he has combined the systems of the two; at the same time, with astonishing and carefully studied elegance,

---

10 I, xiv, pp. 34–35; II, xxix, pp. 140–141 (Bohn's translation, pp. 26–27, 107).

11 Josquin treats the plainsong (*Grad. Rom.*, p. 242) as a "wandering cantus firmus," giving Stanza 1 to the tenor and, in Stanza 2, line 1 to the alto, line 2 to the bass, line 3 to the tenor, and so forth.

12 It is the superius of Ockeghem's chanson "D'un autre amer" (Eugénie Droz, *Trois chansonniers français*, I [Paris, 1927], 72–73).

13 It is the superius of Heyne's chanson "De tous biens plaine" (Knud Jeppesen, *Der Kopenhagener Chansonnier* [Copenhagen, 1927], pp. 7–8).

14 That is, without interpolating the Gregorian Credo, officially of Mode IV, but assigned by Glarean (II, xvii, pp. 104–109, Bohn's translation, pp. 82–86) to the Aeolian mode.

15 Hugo Riemann, *Handbuch der Musikgeschichte*, II, 1 (Leipzig, 1907), 258–268.

he has thrown the phrase [16] into violent disorder, usurping now the leap of the Lydian, now that of the Ionian, until at length, by means of these most beautiful refinements, he glides, creeping unobserved and without offending the ear, from Dorian to Phrygian. That this is difficult to do, especially in these two modes, the Dorian and Phrygian, we have already shown.[17] Thus, contrary to the nature of the modes, he has ended the combined systems of the Dorian and Hypodorian on E, the seat of the Phrygian. Yet there are other compositions in which he has done this also (nor is he alone in it), evidently from an immoderate love of novelty and an excessive eagerness to win a little glory for being unusual, a fault to which the more ingenious professors of the arts are in general so much given that, be it ever so peculiar to the symphonists, they still share it in common with many others. None the less the motet remains between A and d, respecting the limits of the Dorian and Hypodorian systems. And although by his unusual procedure he has sought nothing else, he has at least made it plain that, through the force of his temperament, he could bring it about that the charge customarily brought against the ancient musicians, namely, of progressing "From Dorian to Phrygian," [18] would be brought in vain against him by whom it was so learnedly accomplished, without the slightest offense to the ear. But enough of this motet.[19]

The second combination is that of the Hypophrygian and Phrygian modes, extending from B to e. But the combination rarely descends in this way to B without descending also to A; thus it usually lies between C and e. Yet our Josquin, in setting the Genealogy of Christ Our Saviour according to the Evangelists Matthew and Luke for four voices in harmony in this combination, descends to A re and ascends to f, adding here a semitone and there a tone, and this with his usual license.[20] The first one, according to Matthew, he has arranged in accordance with the true final close of the mode, namely on E; we show it here. The second one, taken from Luke, he has forced to end on G, but without

16 The word "phrase" (*phrasis*) has for Glarean the special meaning "melodic idiom"; the "phrase" of a given mode consists for him partly in its tendency to emphasize its natural arithmetic or harmonic division at the fourth or fifth, partly in its use of certain characteristic tone-successions taken over from plainsong. Compare I, xiii, pp. 32–33 (Bohn's translation, pp. 24–25), where the leaps characteristic of the eight modes of plainsong are discussed and illustrated, also II, xxxvi (Bohn's translation, pp. 119–122). The leap characteristic of the Lydian mode is that from a to c; by "Ionian" leap Glarean must mean that from E to G.

17 II, xi, pp. 90–93 (Bohn's translation, pp.

70–73), where the present example is also mentioned.

18 Ἀπὸ δορίου ἐπὶ φρύγιον. Reinach, in his edition of Plutarch's *De musica* (Paris, 1900, p. 143, note on § 366), suggests that this proverb may be connected with the anecdote of the "Mysians" preserved by Aristotle (*S.R.* I, 23).

19 Despite the range of its tenor, by which Glarean has evidently been misled, Josquin's "De profundis" is clearly Hypophrygian, or combined Phrygian and Hypophrygian; cf. Zarlino, *Istituzioni armoniche* (Venice, 1589), IV, xxiii.

20 *Werken, Motetten,* I (Amsterdam, 1926), 59–69 (Matthew), 70–81 (Luke). The tenor descends to A in the Luke genealogy only.

altering the phrase of the modes at the time, and this also with his usual license.[21] The motet has great majesty, and it is wonderful that from material so sterile, namely, from a bare catalogue of men, he has been able to fashion as many delights as though it had been some fertile narrative. Many other things might be said, but let some of these be left for others to discuss.

The third combination, that of Lydian and Hypolydian, is unusual in this our age, for, as we have often remarked in the foregoing, all compositions in these modes are forced into the Ionian.[22] But in our example, the Agnus Dei from the *Missa Fortuna desperata*,[23] the reader may first admire the way in which a Lydian has been made from an Ionian, for the whole mass is sung in the Ionian mode. This is doubtless due to the bass, plunged into the lowest diapason. For in other compositions, as often as the tenor is Hypodorian, the bass is usually Dorian or Aeolian; again, just as a Phrygian tenor often has an Aeolian bass and cantus, here an Ionian bass has a Lydian tenor and alto.[24] But it is doubtful whether the author has done this by design or by accident. Aside from this, he talks nonsense with his canon, following the custom of the singers.[25] For who except Oedipus himself would understand such a riddle of the sphinx? He has humored the common singers, obeying the maxim, Ἀλωπεκίζειν πρὸς ἑτέραν ἀλώπεκα; that is, *Cum vulpe vulpinare tu quoque invicem*, as Master Erasmus has learnedly translated it, or, as the vulgar inelegantly put it, "Howl with the wolves, if you want to get along with them."

The fourth combination is that of the Mixolydian and its plagal, the Hypomixolydian; in our age it is seldom used. Nevertheless, once the symphonists had perceived the magnificence of these modes from ancient examples of ecclesiastical melody, roused as it were with enthusiasm,

---

21 On this ending see II, xxxvi, p. 163 (Bohn's translation, p. 121), also Pietro Aron, *Trattato della natura et cognizione*. v (pp. 24–25 above).

22 Cf. Pietro Aron, *op. cit.*, vi (p. 25 above).

23 Josquin Desprez, *Werken, Missen*, I (Amsterdam, 1926), 81–104.

24 Cf. III, xiii, pp. 250–251 (Bohn's translation, pp. 197–198), on the "mysterious relationship" of the modes, in which connection the present example is also mentioned. Here, as there, Glarean clearly has three distinct sorts of relationship in mind: (1) the natural relationship of any authentic mode to the plagal mode having the same final; (2) the special relationship of Phrygian to Aeolian, as a result of which a Phrygian composition may have marked Aeolian characteristics or an Aeolian composition a Phrygian final cadence; as an example of this relationship Glarean gives in III, xix, the motet "Tulerunt Dominum meum" (score in Bohn's translation,

pp. 272–278); cf. also Zarlino, *Istituzioni armoniche*. IV, xxx (pages 63–64 below); (3) the peculiar relationship of D-Dorian to D-Aeolian (transposed Aeolian) and of F-Lydian to F-Ionian (transposed Ionian), of which the present example is an illustration.

25 In Agnus I the bass is to invert his part, beginning it an eleventh lower than written and multiplying the time-values by four (double augmentation). Petrucci's editions, followed by Glarean, hint at this in the following distich, which Glarean heads "the riddle of the sphinx":

In gradus undenos descendant multiplicantes
Consimilique modo crescant Antipodes uno.

Let them descend by eleven steps with multiplied measure;
Then once more in like manner increase, to antipodes changing.

they tried in a certain most praiseworthy rivalry to do their utmost with the melody "Et in terra pax" on the Most Blessed Virgin and Queen of Heaven, Mary, Mother of Jesus Christ,[26] above all Antoine Brumel [27] and our Josquin Desprez, at a time when both were verging toward extreme old age.[28] Brumel, in his setting, has spared no pains to show the singers his skill, nay, he has strained every fibre of his temperament to leave behind for later generations a specimen of his ingenuity. Yet, in my opinion at least, Josquin has by far surpassed him in natural force and ingenious penetration and has so borne himself in the contest that Nature, mother of all, as though wishing to form from the four elements her most perfect creation, seems to me to have brought her utmost powers into play in order that it might be impossible to invent a better music. And thus the majority of the learned have not hesitated to award the first place to this composition, especially Joannes Vannius, whom we have mentioned in connection with the Hypomixolydian mode and to whose judgment we gladly subscribe, both because he gave it before us and because he outdid us in this matter by far. At the beginning, the tenor descends once to the Hypomixolydian diatessaron, otherwise the entire melody is Mixolydian, not Hypomixolydian. To me, the greatest passion seems to have been expressed at the word "Primogenitus" in the first part of the setting; others prefer the second part. But there is no part whatever that does not contain something that you may greatly admire.

Of the fifth combination, that of Aeolian and Hypoaeolian, we should not again be giving the same example if we had been able to obtain or discover another one anywhere among the symphonists of our age. Although in our previous book [29] we also produced other examples of the combination, this one [30] was by far the most enlightening, as one by many treated yet by all perverted and transposed from its natural position, even mutilated or altered with respect to its two diatessarons above and below, namely by Brumel and Josquin in their two so celebrated masses of the Virgin Mary, Mother of God; for this reason we have earnestly entreated that excellent man, Master Gregor Meyer, the distinguished organist of the cathedral at Solothurn in Switzerland, to treat the theme worthily, with all the skill at his command, in its natural position and with the two diatessarons proper to and born with the body of the melody.

26 *Grad. Rom.*, p. 32*.

27 Edited by Henry Expert (Paris, 1898) in the series *Maîtres musiciens de la renaissance française.*

28 *Das Chorwerk,* VIII (Wolfenbüttel, 1936), Heft 42.

29 III, xviii, p. 304 (Bohn's translation, p. 259).

30 The Gregorian Kyrie "Cum jubilo" (*Grad. Rom.*, p. 32*), which Glarean has already discussed in II, xxxiii, pp. 152–156 (Bohn's translation, pp. 113–116).

In truth, we imagine this melody to be some splendid bird, whose body is the diapente re-la and whose two wings are the diatessarons mi-la. To sew to this body wings other than those with which it was born would be foolish, surely, unless like Aesop's crow it was to fly with strange plumage. We have prevailed upon him and, in all friendliness toward me and readiness to further liberal studies, he has sent us what we wanted; of this we now desire to make the reader a sharer. We do not at all hesitate to insert this composition among those of Josquin, such praise has been given to it; namely, the opinion of that learned man, Master John Alus, canon of the same cathedral and preacher of the Divine Word, who thinks that it would be no small ornament to the more serious studies, such as theology and sacred letters, if to these were added a knowledge of languages and of the mathematical disciplines, and that among these last it would most befit a priest of Holy Church if he knew music. Nor was the man mistaken in his opinion, for he had become versed in musical knowledge. We had his support in this work when he lived with us at Freiburg at the foot of the Black Forest and often refreshed us, now playing the organ, now joining to this the singing of things by Josquin. And so, since he has given the highest praise to this composition of our Gregor, he has easily won our approval and has been responsible for its coming into men's hands as worthy of the ears of the learned.

Of the sixth combination, that of Hyperaeolian and Hyperphrygian, we have deliberately omitted an example, for none is to be found anywhere and it would be foolish to invent one, especially with so great a choice of modes; the tenor, too, would have an outrageous ambitus, actually exceeding all the remaining combinations of the modes by an apotome. Aside from this, in our previous book we have given an invented example, less for imitation than for illustration, so that the matter might be understood, not so that something of the sort might be attempted by anyone, a thing we find that no one has attempted.

Of the seventh and last combination, namely of Ionian and Hypoionian, our example, "Planxit autem David," is again by Josquin Desprez,[31] the author of the examples of all the other combinations except the fifth. Of its beginning some will no doubt exclaim: "The mountain has labored and brought forth a mouse!" But they will not have considered that, throughout the motet, there is preserved what befits the mourner, who is wont at first to cry out frequently, then to murmur to himself, turning little by little to sorrowful complaints, thereupon

---

[31] *Werken, Motetten,* I (Amsterdam, 1926), 95–104.

to subside or sometimes, when passion breaks out anew, to raise his voice again, shouting out a cry. All these things we see most beautifully observed in this composition, as will be evident to the attentive reader. Nor is there in it anything unworthy of its author; by the gods, he has everywhere expressed the passion in a wonderful way, thus, at the very beginning of the tenor, at the word "Jonathan."

6. Gioseffe Zarlino

Gioseffe Zarlino, easily the most influential personality in the history of musical theory from Aristoxenus to Rameau, was born at Chioggia, not far from Venice, in 1517. His teacher was the Venetian master Adrian Willaert, choirmaster at St. Mark's from 1527 to 1562. In 1565, on the departure for Parma of Cipriano Rore, his fellow-pupil and Willaert's successor, Zarlino fell heir to his old teacher's position at St. Mark's, a position that he continued to occupy until his death in 1590. The *Istituzioni armoniche*, his principal work, first published in 1558, was reprinted in 1562 and 1573; other writings are the *Dimostrazioni armoniche* (1571) and the *Sopplimenti musicali* (1588), this last in reply to the stand taken by Vincenzo Galilei, a rebellious pupil who had attacked Zarlino's entire teaching in his *Dialogo della musica antica e della moderna* (1581).

A true son of the Renaissance, Zarlino paints an ideal picture of the music of the Ancient World, takes pride in what his own time has done to create it anew, and flatly rejects the music of the Middle Ages, which seems to him a species of artistic sophistry. Professing to be more interested in the formulation of basic principles than in the laying-down of rules to govern particular cases, he looks on music as an imitation of nature and endeavors to derive his teachings from natural law. Starting from the ratios for the primary consonances, he succeeds in arriving at many of the conclusions that modern theory draws from the harmonic series, a phenomenon unknown to Zarlino and his time. He was the first to grasp the full implications of just intonation and to produce classical authority for it, the first to deal with harmony in terms of the triad rather than of the interval, the first to recognize the importance of the fundamental antithesis of major and minor, the first to attempt a rational explanation of the old rule forbidding the use of parallel fifths and octaves, the first to isolate and to describe the effects of the false relation; it was at his suggestion that the first printed edition of the *Harmonics* of Aristoxenus (in Latin translation) was undertaken. His writings bear witness to the extraordinary range and depth of his reading and to the understanding with which he read.

From the Istituzioni armoniche [1]

[1558]

Book Three

26. WHAT IS SOUGHT IN EVERY COMPOSITION; AND FIRST, OF THE SUBJECT [2]

I SHALL come now to the discussion of counterpoint, but before I begin this discussion it must be understood that in every good counterpoint, or in every good composition, there are required many things, and one may say that it would be imperfect if one of them were lacking.

The first of these is the subject, without which one can do nothing. For just as the builder, in all his operations, looks always toward the end and founds his work upon some matter which he calls the subject, so the musician in his operations, looking toward the end which prompts him to work, discovers the matter or subject upon which he founds his composition. Thus he perfects his work in conformity with his chosen end. Or again, just as the poet, prompted by such an end to improve or to delight (as Horace shows so clearly in his *Art of Poetry*, when he says:

Aut prodesse volunt, aut delectare poetae
Aut simul et iucunda et idonea dicere vitae), [3]

takes as the subject of his poem some history or fable, discovered by himself or borrowed from others, which he adorns and polishes with various manners, as he may prefer, leaving out nothing that might be fit or worthy to delight the minds of his hearers, in such a way that he takes on something of the magnificent and marvelous; so the musician, apart from being prompted by the same end to improve or to delight the minds of his listeners with harmonious accents, takes the subject and founds upon it his composition, which he adorns with various modulations and various harmonies in such a way that he offers welcome pleasure to his hearers.

---

1 Text: The edition published as the first volume of the *Opere* (Venice, 1589), collated with the first and second editions (Venice, 1558 and 1562). The postils of the original and some of the additions of 1589 are given as author's notes. For the title page in facsimile, see Kinsky, p. 110, Fig. 5.

2 The first half of this chapter is literally translated by Cerone in his *Melopeo* (Naples, 1613), XII, i.

8 Lines 333-334. "Poets aim either to benefit, or to amuse, or to utter words at once both pleasing and helpful to life." [Fairclough]

The second condition is that the composition should be principally composed of consonances; in addition, it should incidentally include many dissonances, suitably arranged in accordance with the rules which I propose to give later on.

The third is that the procedure of the parts should be good, that is, that the modulations [4] should proceed by true and legitimate intervals arising from the sonorous numbers,[5] so that through them may be acquired the usage of good harmonies.

The fourth condition to be sought is that the modulations and the concentus be varied, for harmony [6] has no other source than the diversity of the modulations and the diversity of the consonances variously combined.

The fifth is that the composition should be subject to a prescribed and determined harmony, mode, or tone (call it as we will), and that it should not be disordered.

The sixth and last (aside from the others which might be added) is that the harmony it contains should be so adapted to the speech, that is, to the words, that in joyous matters the harmony will not be mournful, and vice versa, that in mournful ones the harmony will not be joyful.

To assure a perfect understanding of the whole, I shall discuss these things separately as they become suited to my purpose and to my needs.

Beginning with the first, then, I say that, in every musical composition, what we call the subject is that part from which the composer derives

---

[4] "A movement made from one sound to another by means of various intervals" (II, xiv). Zarlino distinguishes two sorts of modulation: "improper," as in plainsong, and "proper," as in figured music. "Proper modulation" has these further divisions: first, sol-fa or solmization; second, the modulation of artificial instruments; third, modulation in which words are adapted to the musical figures.

[5] "Sonorous number is number related to voices and to sounds" (I, xix). For Zarlino, the sonorous (or harmonic) numbers are specifically the numbers 1 to 6, with their products and their squares. As he says in I, xv, the six-part number has its parts so proportioned that, when any two of them are taken, their relation gives us the ratio or form of one of the musical consonances, simple or composite. And these parts are so ordered that, if we take six strings stretched subject to the ratio of the numbers 1 to 6, when we strike them all together, our ear perceives no discrepancy and takes the highest pleasure in the harmony that arises; the opposite is the case if the order is changed in any respect. It should be noted that Zarlino does not say that the lengths of the strings correspond to the numbers 1 to 6; he says that they correspond to the ratios of these numbers. The relative lengths, as given in the *Dimostrazioni armoniche*, III, *Definizione* xliv, are 60, 30, 20, 15, 12, and 10; the resulting harmony will consist of unison,

octave, twelfth, fifteenth, seventeenth, and nineteenth.

[6] In II, xii, Zarlino defines harmony as having two varieties, "proper" and "improper." "Proper harmony" is a combination or mixture of low and high sounds, divided or not divided by intermediate sounds, which impresses the ear agreeably; it arises from the parts of a composition through the procedure which they make in accord with one another until they attain their end, and it has the power to dispose the soul to various passions. "Proper harmony" arises not only from consonances, but also from dissonances. It has two divisions: "perfect," as in the singing of many parts, and "imperfect," as in the singing of two parts only. "Improper harmony" arises when two sounds distant from one another with respect to the low and the high are heard divided by other intermediate sounds so that they give out an agreeable concentus, subject to several proportions. Musicians call such a combination a harmony. But, Zarlino says, it ought rather to be called a harmonious consonance, for it contains no modulation, and although its extremes are divided, it has no power to move the soul. "Improper harmony" has also two divisions: "simple," as in a combination of consonances arranged in harmonic proportion, and "by extension of meaning" (*ad un certo modo*), as in a combination otherwise arranged.

the invention to make the other parts of the work, however many they may be. Such a subject may take many forms, as the composer may prefer and in accordance with the loftiness of his imagination: it may be his own invention, that is, it may be that he has discovered it of himself; again, it may be that he has borrowed it from the works of others, adapting it to his work and adorning it with various parts and various modulations. And such a subject may be of several kinds: it may be a tenor or some other part of any composition you please, whether of plainsong or of figured music; again, it may be two or more parts of which one follows another in consequence [7] or in some other way, for the various forms of such subjects are innumerable.

When the composer has discovered his subject, he will write the other parts in the way which we shall see later on. When this is done, our practical musicians call the manner of composing "making counterpoint."

But when the composer has not first discovered his subject, that part which he first puts into execution or with which he begins his work, whatever it may be or however it may begin, whether high, low, or intermediate, will always be the subject to which he will then adapt the other parts in consequence or in some other way, as he prefers, adapting the harmony to the words as the matter they contain demands. And when the composer goes on to derive the subject from the parts of the work, that is, when he derives one part from another and goes on to write the work all at once, as we shall see elsewhere, that small part which he derives without the others and upon which he then composes the parts of his composition will always be called the subject. This manner of composing practical musicians call "composing from fantasy," although it may also be called "counterpointing," or as they say, "making counterpoint."

. . . . . .

27. THAT COMPOSITIONS SHOULD BE MADE UP PRIMARILY OF CONSONANCES, AND SECONDARILY AND INCIDENTALLY OF DISSONANCES

And although every composition, every counterpoint, and in a word every harmony is made up primarily and principally of consonances, dis-

---

7 "Consequence we define as a certain repetition or return of a part or the whole of a modulation; it arises from an order and arrangement of many musical figures which the composer makes in one part of his composition and from which, after a certain and limited space of time, there follow one or more other parts, low, high, intermediate, or in the same sound, at the diapa- son, diapente, diatessaron, or unison, these proceeding one after another by the same intervals. Imitation we shall define as a repetition or return which does not proceed by the same intervals but by wholly different ones, only the movements made by the parts and the figures being similar" (III, liv). Each has two varieties, strict and free, and may be either in direct or in contrary motion.

sonances are used secondarily and incidentally for the sake of greater beauty and elegance. Taken by themselves, these are not very acceptable to the ear; arranged as they regularly should be and in accordance with the precepts which we shall give, the ear tolerates them to such an extent that, far from being offended, it receives from them great pleasure and delight.

From this, among many other advantages, the musician derives two of no little value: we have already stated the first, namely, that with their aid he may pass from one consonance to another; [8] the second is that a dissonance causes the consonance which immediately follows it to seem more acceptable. Thus it is perceived and recognized with greater pleasure by the ear, just as after darkness light is more acceptable and delightful to the eye, and after the bitter the sweet is more luscious and palatable. And from everyday experience with sounds we learn that if a dissonance offends the ear for a certain length of time, the consonance which follows is made more acceptable and more sweet.

Thus the ancient musicians judged that they should admit in composition not only the consonances which they called perfect and those which they called imperfect, but dissonances also, knowing that their compositions would thus attain to greater beauty and elegance than they would without them. For if they were made up entirely of consonances, although beautiful sounds and good effects would issue from them, they would still be somehow imperfect, both as sound and as composition, seeing that (the consonances not being blended with dissonances) they would lack the great elegance that dissonance affords.

And although I have said that the composer is to use consonances principally and dissonances incidentally, he is not to understand by this that he is to use them in his counterpoints or compositions as they come to hand, without any rule or any order, for this would lead to confusion; on the contrary, he must take care to use them in a regular and orderly manner so that the whole will be profitable. Above all (apart from other things) he must keep in mind the two considerations upon which (in my judgment) all the beauty, all the elegance, and all the excellence of music depend: the movements which the parts of the composition make in ascending or descending in similar or contrary motion, and the arrangement of the consonances in their proper places in the harmonies. Of these things I propose with God's help to speak as may suit my purpose, for this has always been my chief intention.

And to introduce this discussion I propose to explain certain rules laid

---

[8] III, xvii.

down by the ancients, who recognized the importance of such matters; teaching by means of these the regular procedure to be followed in using the consonances and dissonances one after another in composition, they went on to give rules about the movements, which they did imperfectly. Thus I shall state and explain these rules in order, and from this explanation I shall go on to show with evident reason what is to be done and how the rules are to be understood, adding also certain further rules, not only useful but also most necessary to those who seek to train themselves in a regular and well-ordered way of composing music of any kind in a learned and elegant manner, with good reasons and good foundations. In this way everyone may know in what part to arrange the consonances and in what place to use the major and the minor in his compositions.

· · · · ·

29. THAT TWO CONSONANCES SUBJECT TO THE SAME PROPORTION ARE NOT TO BE USED ONE AFTER ANOTHER, ASCENDING OR DESCENDING, WITHOUT A MEAN [9]

The ancient composers also avoided using one after another two perfect consonances of the same genus or species, their extremes subject to the same proportion, the modulations moving one step or more; thus they avoided using two or more unisons, two or more octaves, or two or more fifths, as seen in the following examples:

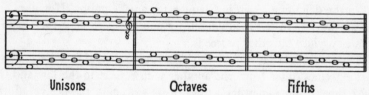

Unisons   Octaves   Fifths

For they knew very well that harmony can arise only from things that are among themselves diverse, discordant, and contrary, and not from things that are in complete agreement. Now if harmony arises from variety such as this, it is not sufficient that in music the parts of the composition be at a distance from one another with respect to the low and the high; the modulations must also be varied in their movements and must contain various consonances, subject to various proportions. And the more harmonious we judge a composition to be, the more we will find, between its several parts, different distances with respect to the

---

[9] Having concluded the discussion of his first and second requirements, Zarlino now skips over to the fourth, leaving the third for Chapters 30 and 31.

low and the high, different movements, and different proportions. Perhaps the ancients saw that when consonances were not put together in the manner I have described, they were similar in their procedure and similar in the form of their proportions, although sometimes varied in their extremes with respect to the low and the high. Knowing, then, that such similarity can generate no variety in the concentus and judging (as was true) that perfect harmony consists in variety, not so much in the positions or distances of the parts of the composition as in the movements, the modulations, and the proportions, they held that in taking one after another two consonances similar in proportion, they were varying the position from low to high, or vice versa, without producing any good harmony, even though the extremes did vary one from another. Thus they did not wish that in composition two or more perfect consonances subject to the same proportion should be taken one after another, the parts ascending or descending together, without the mediation of another interval.

The unisons they especially avoided, for these sounds have no extremes and are neither different in position, nor at a distance from one another, nor productive of any variety in the procedure, but wholly similar in every respect. Nor in singing them does one find any difference with respect to the low and the high, for there is no interval between the one sound and the other, the sounds of the one part being in the same places as those of the other, as may be seen in the example above and in the definition given in Chapter 11, on the unison. Nor does one find any variety in the modulation, for the one part sings the very intervals by which the other proceeds.

The same might be said of two or more octaves, if it were not that their extremes differ from one another with respect to the low and the high; thus, being somewhat varied in its extremes, the octave affords the ear somewhat more pleasure than the unison.

And the same may be said of two or more fifths; since these progress by similar steps and proportions, some of the ancients were of the opinion that to a certain extent they gave rise rather to dissonance than to harmony or consonance.

Thus they held it as true that whenever one had arrived at perfect consonance one had attained the end and the perfection toward which music tends, and in order not to give the ear too much of this perfection they did not wish it repeated over and over again.

The truth and excellence of this admirable and useful admonition are confirmed by the operations of Nature, for in bringing into being the individuals of each species she makes them similar to one another in general, yet different in some particular, a difference or variety affording much pleasure to our senses. This admirable order the composer ought to imitate, for the more his operations resemble those of our great mother, the more he will be esteemed. And to this course the numbers and proportions invite him, for in their natural order one will not find two similar proportions following one another immediately, such as the progressions 1:1:1 or 2:2:2 or others like them, which would give the forms of two unisons, still less the progression 1:2:4:8, which is not harmonic but geometric and would give the forms of three consecutive octaves, and still less the progression 4:6:9, which would give the forms of two consecutive fifths. Thus he ought under no conditions to take one after another two unisons, or two octaves, or two fifths, since the natural cause of the consonances, which is the harmonic number, does not in its progression or natural order contain two similar proportions one after another without a mean, as may be seen in Chapter 15 of Part I. For although these consonances, taken in this manner, would obviously cause no dissonance between the parts, a certain heaviness would be heard which would displease.

For all these reasons, then, we ought under no conditions to offend against this rule, that is, we ought never to use the consonances one after another in the way described above; on the contrary, we should seek always to vary the sounds, the consonances, the movements, and the intervals, and in this way, from the variety of these things, we shall come to make a good and perfect harmony. Nor need it concern us that some have sought to do the opposite, rather (as we see from their compositions) from presumption and on their own authority than for any reason that they have had. For we ought not to imitate those who offend impertinently against the good manners and good rules of an art or science without giving any reason for doing so; we ought to imitate those who have conformed, conforming ourselves to them and embracing them as good masters, always avoiding the dreary and taking the good. And I say this for this reason: just as the sight of a picture is more delightful to the eye when it is painted with various colors than when it is painted with one color only, so the ear takes more pleasure and delight in the varied consonances which the more diligent composer puts into his compositions than in the simple and unvaried.

This the more diligent ancient musicians, to whom we are so much indebted, wished observed, and to it we add that, for the reasons already given, the composer ought not to use two or more imperfect consonances one after another, ascending or descending together, without a mean, such as two major or minor thirds, or two major or minor sixths, as seen in the example:

Major thirds   Minor thirds   Major sixths   Minor sixths

For not only do these offend against what I have said about the perfect consonances, but their procedure causes a certain bitterness to be heard, since there is altogether lacking in their modulations the interval of the major semitone, in which lies all the good in music and without which every modulation and every harmony is harsh, bitter, and as it were inconsonant. Another reason for this bitterness is that there is no harmonic relationship [10] between the parts or sounds of two major thirds or of two minor sixths, which makes these somewhat more dreary than the others, as we shall see later on. Thus in every progression or modulation which the parts make in singing together we ought to take special care that wherever possible at least one of them has or moves by the interval of the major semitone, so that the modulation and the harmony which arise from the movements which the parts of the composition make together may be more delightful and more sweet.[11] This is easily managed if the consonances taken one after another are diverse in species, so that after the major third or sixth will follow the minor, or vice versa, or so that after the major third will follow the minor sixth, or after the latter the former, and after the minor third the major sixth, or in the same way after the major sixth the minor third.[12] Nor is there more reason for forbidding the use, one after another, of two perfect consonances than of two imperfect ones, for although the former are perfect consonances, each of the latter is found to be perfect in its proportion. And just as it may not be said with truth that one man is more man than another, so also it may not be said that a major or minor third

---

10 Non-harmonic relationship or, as we should call it, false relation is defined and discussed in Chapters 30 and 31.

11 "The semitone is indeed the salt (so to speak), the condiment, and the cause of every good modulation and every good harmony" (III, x, with reference to the role of the semitone in the progressions major sixth to octave, major third to fifth, minor sixth to fifth, minor third to unison). "Guido places the semitone in the

center of each of his hexachords, as though in the most worthy and most honored place, the seat of Virtue (as they say), for its excellence and nobility are such that without it every composition would be harsh and unbearable to hear, nor can one have any perfect harmony except by means of it" (III, xix).

12 As in the first part of the musical example at the top of p. 48 below.

or sixth taken below is greater or less than another taken above, or vice versa. Thus, since it is forbidden to use two perfect consonances of the same species one after another, we ought still less to use two imperfect ones of the same proportion, seeing that they are less consonant than the perfect.

But when two minor thirds, and similarly two major sixths, are used one after another, ascending or descending together by step, they may be tolerated, for although the major semitone is not heard in their modulations, and the thirds are naturally somewhat mournful and the sixths somewhat harsh, the slight difference that is heard in the movements of the parts gives a certain variety. For the lower part always ascends or descends by a minor tone and the upper by a major, or vice versa,[13] and this affords a certain satisfaction to the ear, the more so since the sounds of the parts stand in a harmonic relationship to one another. But when the parts move by leap we ought by no means to use two or more similar consonances one after another, ascending or descending, for apart from not observing the conditions touched on above, the sounds of the parts will not stand in a harmonic relationship to one another, as seen below:

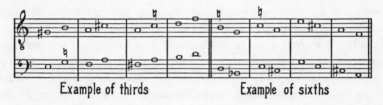

Example of thirds   Example of sixths

Thus, to avoid the errors that may occur when it becomes necessary to take two thirds or two sixths one after another, we shall take care to take first the major and then the minor, or vice versa, taking them in whatever manner we wish, with movements by step or by leap, for everything will now agree. And we ought also to take care that, in taking the third after the sixth or the sixth after the third, we make one of them major and the other minor, as we can when there is movement in each of the parts, above and below. But when there is no movement in one or other of them, this rule cannot be observed without departing from the rules which, for the well-being of the composition, we shall give later on. Thus after the major third we shall have to take the major sixth and after the minor third the minor sixth, or vice versa, as seen in the example below:

13 In Zarlino's scale the minor tones are those from d to e and from g to a, all the others are major, including the tone b-flat to c.

Example of everything that has been said

We shall add that, it being forbidden to take two perfect or imperfect consonances in the way we have described, we ought also not to take two fourths in any composition whatever, as some do in certain short sections of their *canzoni* which they call *falso bordone*, for the fourth is without a doubt a perfect consonance.[14] But I shall discuss this point when I show how to compose for more than two voices.

30. WHEN THE PARTS OF A CANTILENA HAVE BETWEEN THEM A HARMONIC RELATIONSHIP, AND HOW WE MAY USE THE SEMIDIAPENTE AND THE TRITONE IN COMPOSITION

Before going on, I propose to explain what I have said above about the parts of the composition, namely, that sounds sometimes have and sometimes have not a harmonic relationship between them. It must first be understood that to say that the parts of a composition do not have between them a harmonic relationship is to say that between two consonances that two parts make one after another in singing, ascending or descending together, or ascending and descending together, there comes to be heard the augmented diapason, or the semidiapente, or the tritone. This occurs in the crossing of the first figure or note of the upper part with the second figure or note of the lower, or of the first of the lower with the second of the upper. Such a relationship, then, can occur only when we have at least four figures or notes, namely, the two lower and the two upper figures or notes of two consonances, as seen here:[a]

Augmented   Semidiapason   Semidiapente   Tritones
diapason

---

a But when two parts ascend together and the one or the other makes a movement which involves the semitone, it seems that because of this movement they are tolerated by the ear, as are the first cases of the augmented diapason and the semidiapente in the first and third sections of the example. [This sentence is not found in earlier editions of the *Istituzioni* and has accordingly been made a note.—Ed.]

14 III, lxi. "I am well aware that with many the authority of those who have taken this liberty

Thus, in order that our compositions may be correct and purged of every error, we shall seek to avoid these relationships as much as we can, especially when we compose for two voices, since these give rise to a certain fastidiousness in discriminating ears. For intervals like these do not occur among the sonorous numbers and are not sung in any sort of composition, even though some have held a contrary opinion. But be this as it may, they are most difficult to sing and they make a dreary effect.

And I am much astonished by those who have not hesitated at all to require the singing or modulation of these intervals in the parts of their compositions, and I cannot imagine why they have done so. And although it is not so bad to find this in the relationship between two modulations as to find it in the modulation of a single part, the same evil that was heard in the single part is now heard divided between two, and it gives the same offense to the ear. For unless the evil is diminished, little or nothing relieves the offensive nature of a fault, even though it be more offensive from one than from many.

Thus, in a composition for several voices, those intervals that are not admitted in modulation are to be so avoided that they will not be heard as relationships between the parts. This will have been done when the parts can be interchanged by means of harmonically proportioned intervals of the diatonic genus, that is, when we can ascend from the first sound of the lower part to the following sound of the upper, or vice versa, by a legitimate and singable interval. But this will not be the case when non-harmonic relationships are heard between the parts of the composition, whatever it may be, among four sounds arranged in the manner explained, for these cannot be changed unless with great disadvantage, as the intervals of the last example are changed in the example below:

Changes of the parts given above

Thus, whenever the parts of a composition or cantilena cannot be so interchanged that from this change there arises a procedure by true and legitimate singable intervals, we ought to avoid it, especially if our compositions are to be correct and purged of every error. But in composi-

will count more than the arguments I have put forward against it; let them do their worst by saying that what I hold in little esteem has been practised by many, for they are not capable of reason and do not wish to be."

tions for more than two voices it is often impossible to avoid such things and not to run into intricacies of this kind. For it sometimes happens that the composer will write upon a subject which repeatedly invites him to offend against this precept; thus, when necessity compels him, he will ignore it, as when he sees that the parts of his composition cannot be sung with comfort or when he wishes to adapt a consequent which may be sung with comfort, as we shall see elsewhere.[15] But when necessity compels him to offend, he ought at least to take care that he does so between diatonic steps and in steps which are natural and proper to the mode, for these do not give rise to so dreary an effect as do those which are accidental, being indicated within the composition by the signs ♮, ♯, and ♭.

Take note that I call those errors "natural" which arise in the way shown in the first example above, and that I call those "accidental" which arise when, between the true steps of the mode, there is inserted a step of another order, this step being the cause of the difficulty, as may happen in the Fifth Mode,[16] where the central step ♮ is often rejected in favor of the accidental ♭. Thus, between the ♭ and the ♮ preceding or following it, there will arise some one of the disorders in question, as seen in the first of the examples below. And this is the less agreeable since the ♮, which is the principal step of the mode, is absent from its proper place while the ♭, which is accidental, is present in its stead.

And although, for the reasons already given, we ought not to use these intervals in composition in this way, we may sometimes use the semidiapente as a single percussion if immediately after it we come to the ditone, for, as seen in the third of the examples below, the parts may be interchanged without disadvantage. This the better modern musicians observe, just as some of the more ancient observed it in the past.[17] And we are permitted to use not only the semidiapente, but in some cases the tritone also, as we shall see at the proper time. It will, however, be more advantageous to use the semidiapente than the tritone, for the consonances will then stand in their proper places, a thing which will not occur when the tritone is used. And we ought to take care that, in the parts involved, the semidiapente or tritone is immediately preceded by

---

15 III, lv, lxiii.

16 The Third Mode of the ecclesiastical system (Glarean's Phrygian). Having adopted Glarean's twelve modes in the earlier editions of the *Istituzioni* (1558 and 1562), by 1571, when the *Dimostrazioni* were first published, Zarlino had persuaded himself to renumber them, counting the authentic and plagal forms of the C mode as First and Second, and so forth. The various arguments for this renumbering are set forth in the *Dimostrazioni* (V, Def. viii) and summarized by Hölger in his "Bemerkungen zu Zarlinos Theorie," *Zeitschrift für Musikwissenschaft*, IX (1926–27), 518–527. The principal argument is that, in numbering the species of any interval, the point of departure ought to be the natural scale resulting from the harmonic numbers.

17 III, lxi.

a consonance, no matter whether perfect or imperfect, for through the force of the preceding and following consonances the semidiapente comes to be tempered in such a way that, instead of making a dreary effect, it makes a good one, as experience proves and as is heard in the examples that follow.

First example   Second example   Third example

31. WHAT CONSIDERATION IS TO BE PAID TO RELATED INTERVALS IN COMPOSITIONS FOR MORE THAN TWO VOICES

Aside from this, the composer should bear in mind that, when they occur in counterpoints without being combined with other intervals, such relationships as the tritone, the semidiapente, the semidiapason, and the others that are similar to them are counted among the things in music that can afford little pleasure. Thus we should oblige ourselves not to use them in simple compositions, which (as I have said) are those for two voices, or in other compositions when two parts sing alone, for the same effects will obviously be heard in these. This is because there will not in either case be present what we have called "perfect harmony," in which a body of consonances and harmonies is heard, the extreme sounds being divided by other mean sounds; on the contrary, there will be present only what we have called "imperfect harmony," in which only two parts are heard singing together, no other sound dividing.[18] And since the sense of hearing grasps two parts more fully than three or four, we ought to vary the harmony between the two as much as we can and to take care not to use these relationships, a thing which may be done without any difficulty.

But in compositions for more than two voices this consideration is not so necessary, both because we cannot always observe it without great inconvenience, and because variety now consists not only in the changing of consonances, but also in the changing of harmonies and positions, a thing which is not true of compositions for two voices.

And I say this for this reason: just as there are ingredients in medicines and other electuaries, bitter and even poisonous in themselves, but in-

18 For "perfect" and "imperfect" harmony, Zarlino has "proper" and "improper," an obvious slip; cf. note 6, p. 40 above.

dubitably health-giving and less harsh when combined with other ingredients, so many things which in themselves are harsh and harmful become good and healthful when combined with others. Thus it is with these relationships in music. And there are other intervals which in themselves give little pleasure, but when combined with others make marvelous effects.

We ought, then, to consider these relationships in one way when we are about to use them simply and in another when we are about to use them in combination. For the variety of the harmony in such combinations consists not only in the variety of the consonances which occur between the parts, but also in the variety of the harmonies, which arises from the position of the sound forming the third or tenth above the lowest part of the composition. Either this is minor and the resulting harmony is ordered by or resembles the arithmetical proportion or mean, or it is major and the harmony is ordered by or resembles the harmonic.[19]

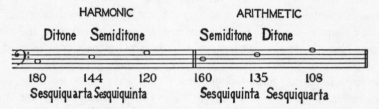

On this variety depend the whole diversity and perfection of the harmonies. For (as I shall say elsewhere) [20] in the perfect composition the fifth and third, or their extensions, must always be actively present, seeing that apart from these two consonances the ear can desire no sound that falls between their extremes or beyond them and yet is wholly distinct and different from those that lie within the extremes of these two consonances combined. For in this combination occur all the different sounds that can form different harmonies. But since the extremes of the fifth are invariable and always placed subject to the same proportion, apart from certain cases in which the fifth is used imperfectly, the extremes of the thirds are given different positions. I do not say different in proportion; I say different in position, for (as I have said elsewhere [b]) when the major third is placed below, the harmony is made joyful and when it is placed above, the harmony is made mournful. Thus, from the dif-

---

[b] Chapter 10.

[19] "Not with respect to the order of the proportions, which is actually arithmetic, but with respect to the proportions of the parts when the mean term has been interposed, for these are of the same quantity and proportion as are those produced by a harmonic mean term or divisor, although in the opposite order." (I, xv.)

[20] III, lix.

ferent positions of the thirds which are placed in counterpoint between the extremes of the fifth or above the octave, the variety of harmony arises.

If, then, we wish to vary the harmony and to observe in so far as possible the rule laid down in Chapter 29 (although this is not so necessary in compositions for more than two voices as it is in those for two) we must take the different thirds in such a way that, after first taking the major third, which forms the harmonic mean, we then take the minor, which forms the arithmetical. This we would not be able to observe so easily if we were to take the non-harmonic relationships into consideration, for while we were seeking to avoid them, we would be continuing the concentus in one division for some time without the mediation of the other; thus to no purpose we would cause the composition to sound mournful to words that carry joyfulness with them or to sound joyful to words that treat of mournful matters. I do not go so far as to say that the composer may not take two arithmetical divisions one after another, but I do say that he ought not to continue in this division for long, since to do so would make the concentus very melancholy. But to take two harmonic divisions one after another can never give offense, provided they be formed from natural steps, and with some judgment and purpose from accidental ones, for when its parts are thus arranged in order, harmony attains its ultimate end and makes its best effect.

But when two parts ascend or descend by one step or two steps we ought to use different divisions, especially when the tritone or semidiapente falls as a relationship between the two parts involved, that is, when in ascending or descending one step two major thirds are taken one after another, and when ascending or descending two steps two minor ones. But when the relationship is that of the semidiatessaron,[21] and it occurs between accidental signs, such as the ♯ and the ♭, or when only one of these signs is present, we need not avoid it at all, for the two divisions being harmonic it is obvious that they will make a good effect, even though they are not varied.

Nor need this astonish anyone, for if he will carefully examine the consonances arranged in the two orders, he will discover that the order which is arithmetical or resembles the arithmetical departs a little from the perfection of harmony, its parts being arranged out of their natural

21 For *semidiatessaron* (diminished fourth) we ought probably to read *diapente superflua* (augmented fifth); diminished fourths, fifths, and octaves occur as false relations between minor consonances, augmented ones between major consonances. Zarlino has already shown how the diminished fourth and augmented fifth occur as false relations in the musical example on p. 47.

Semidiatesseron   Augmented diapente

positions; on the other hand he will discover that the harmony which arises from or resembles the harmonic division is perfectly consonant, its parts being arranged and subject to the proper order of this proportion and according to the order which the sonorous numbers maintain in their natural succession, to be seen in Chapter 15 of Part I.

Let this be enough for the present; at another time, perhaps, I shall touch on this again in order that what I have said may be better understood.

* * * * *

40. THE PROCEDURE TO BE FOLLOWED IN WRITING SIMPLE COUNTERPOINTS FOR TWO VOICES, SUCH AS ARE CALLED NOTE AGAINST NOTE

To come now to the application of the rules that I have given, I shall show the procedure to be followed in writing counterpoints, beginning with those which are written simply and for two voices, note against note. From these the composer may go on to diminished counterpoints and to the usage of other compositions. Wishing then to observe what has been observed by all good writers and compilers on every other subject, I shall with reason begin with simple things, both to make the reader more submissive and to avoid confusion.

First observing what was said above in Chapter 26, the composer will choose a tenor from any plainsong he pleases, and this will be the subject of his composition, that is, of his counterpoint. Then he will examine it carefully and will see in what mode it is composed, so that he may make the appropriate cadences in their proper places and may know from these the nature of his composition. For if inadvertently he were to make these inappropriately and out of their places, mixing those of one mode with those of another, the end of his composition would come to be dissonant with the beginning and the middle.

But assuming that the chosen subject is the plainsong tenor given below, which is subject to the Third Mode,[22] he will above all else observe what was said in Chapter 28 above about the procedure in beginning a composition. Thus we shall place the first figure or note of our counterpoint at such an interval from the first of the subject that they will have between them one of the perfect consonances. This done, we shall combine the second note of our counterpoint with the second of the subject in a consonance, either perfect or imperfect, but in any case different from the preceding one, so that we shall not be offending against what

---

22 The First Mode of the ecclesiastical system (Glarean's Dorian).

was said in Chapter 29, always having an eye to what was laid down in Chapter 38 [23] and observing the teaching of Chapter 37,[24] taking care that the parts of the composition are as conjunct as possible and that they make no large leaps, so that the interval between them will not be too great. This done, we shall come to the third figure or note of our counterpoint and combine it with the third of the subject, varying not only the steps or positions but also the consonances, taking perfect consonance after imperfect, or vice versa, or taking one after another two perfect consonances or two imperfect ones different in species, according to the rules given in Chapter 33 [25] and 34.[26] We shall do the same with the fourth note of our counterpoint and the fourth of the subject, and with the fifth, the sixth, and the others in order until we come to the end, where, following the rule given in the preceding chapter, we shall conclude our counterpoint with one of the perfect consonances.

But above all else we must take care that the contrapuntal part is not only varied in its different movements, touching different steps, now high, now low, and now intermediate, but that it is varied also in its consonances with the subject. And we should see to it that the contrapuntal part sings well and proceeds in so far as possible by step, since there lies in this a part of the beauty of counterpoint. And added to the many other things that one may ask (as we shall see), this will bring it to its perfection.

Thus he who will first exercise himself in this simple manner of composing may afterwards go on easily and quickly to greater things. For seeking to write various counterpoints and compositions upon a single subject, now below and now above, he will make himself thoroughly familiar with the steps and with the intervals of each consonance; then, following the precepts which I am about to give, he will be able to go on to the diminution of the figures, that is, to diminished counterpoint, writing the contrapuntal parts sometimes in consequence with his subject and sometimes imitating them or writing them in other ways, as we shall see; and from this he will be able to go on to compositions for more voices, so that, aided by our directions and by his own talents, he will in a short time become a good composer.

Take note, however, that in laying down a rule governing the procedure to be followed in writing a counterpoint upon a subject, I do

---

23 How we ought to proceed from one consonance to another.

24 That we ought to avoid as much as we can those movements that are made by leap, and in a similar way those distances that may occur between the parts of a composition.

25 When two or more perfect or imperfect consonances, subject to different forms and taken one immediately after another, are conceded.

26 That we do well to take imperfect consonance after perfect, or vice versa.

so, not in particular, but in general. Thus, with those rules which have been given before, the composer must use intelligence in deriving the counterpoint and must work with judgment, and in acquiring this, rules and precepts will have little value unless nature has aided him. Nor need this astonish him at all, seeing that it is true of every art and of every teaching.

For all who have sought to give instruction and to teach any art or science have always laid down general principles, seeing that science has to do, not with particulars, which are innumerable, but with general principles. This we see in the precepts of poetry and of oratory, as set down by Plato, Aristotle, Hermogenes, Demetrius Phalerius, Cicero, Quintilian, Horace, and others besides; these deal with the general and not with the particular. To give an example, I recall what Horace says, speaking in general of the order that poets are to follow in arranging their subject, which is history or fable, in the epic:

> Ordinis haec virtus erit et venus, aut ego fallor,
> Ut iam nunc dicat iam nunc debentia dici,
> Pleraque differat et praesens in tempus omittat.[e]

This rule was most familiar to the learned Virgil, as we shall see. For having chosen a particular subject, which was to describe the fall and burning of Troy and the voyage of Aeneas, he began at once with the voyage, interrupting the order, for the voyage came afterwards. But he understood that his poem would gain in art and in majesty if he were to cause the story to be told by Aeneas in Dido's presence, as he did, taking his occasion from the fortunes that had brought Aeneas to her in Carthage.[d] Such is the custom of the poets, and not only of the poets but also of the painters; these adapt history or fable as may best suit their purpose, for painting is simply silent poetry. Thus the painter, having once undertaken to depict a history or fable, adapts the figures and arranges them in his composition as they seem to him to stand best or to make the best effect, nor does he hesitate to place one of them rather in this way than in that—that is, to cause one of them to stand or to sit rather in one way than in another—as long as he observes the order of the history or fable which he is seeking to represent. And one sees that, although innumerable painters have depicted a single subject in innumerable manners, as I have often seen depicted the story of Roman Lucretia, the wife of Collatinus, the story of Horatius Cocles, and many others, all have had a single aim—that of representing the story. And

c *Ars poetica*, 42–44. ["Of order, this, if I mistake not, will be the excellence and charm: to say at the moment what at that moment should be said, reserving and omitting much for the present."—Fairclough]
d *Aeneid*, II.

one sees this done, not only by various painters of a single subject, but also by the single painter who has depicted a single subject in various ways.

Thus the musician must also seek to vary his counterpoint upon the subject, and if he can invent many passages he will choose the one that is best, most suited to his purpose, and most capable of making his counterpoint sonorous and orderly; the others he will set aside. And when he has invented a passage such as might be appropriate for a cadence, if it is not at the moment to his purpose he will reserve it for some other more suitable place. This he will do if the clause or period in the words or speech has not come to an end, for he must always wait until each of these is finished; in a similar way he will take care that it is in the proper place and that the mode in which his composition stands requires it.

He who wishes to begin in the right way with the art of counterpoint must observe all these things. But above everything else he must industriously exercise himself in this sort of composition in order that he may thus arrive more easily at the practice of diminished counterpoint, in which, as we shall see later on, there are many other things that he may use. And in order that he may have some understanding of all that I have said, I shall give below some varied counterpoints, note against note, upon the subject already mentioned; once he has examined these, he will readily understand the things that I shall show later on [27] and will be able to work with greater ease.

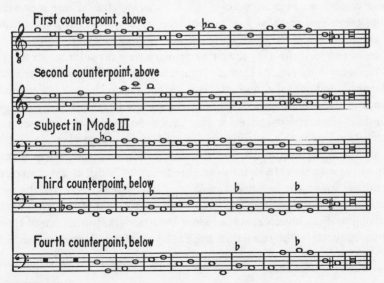

First counterpoint, above

Second counterpoint, above

Subject in Mode III

Third counterpoint, below

Fourth counterpoint, below

---

27 III, xlii–xliv.

Be advised, however, that to write counterpoint, note against note, appears to be and actually is somewhat more difficult than to write it diminished, for the one has not that liberty which the other has, seeing that in the one each note or figure may have one consonance only, while in the other it may have many of them, blended with dissonances according to the composer's pleasure and good judgment. Thus in the first sort the composer cannot at his pleasure arrange the parts so well that they will be without leaps, especially if he wishes to write upon a single subject many counterpoints which will be different throughout. But this need not discourage him, for if the root tastes somewhat bitter, he will before long enjoy the fruits which spring from it, and these are sweet, luscious, and palatable. Thus virtue (as the wise affirm) has to do with the difficult and not with the easy.

· · · · · ·

71. ON THE BENEFIT WHICH GOOD HARMONIES DERIVE FROM THE ACCIDENTS ENUMERATED

And now, before going further, let us determine to what extent good and sonorous harmonies derive benefit from the accidents enumerated.[28] And adopting a somewhat lofty manner of speaking for the sake of greater clarity: if the true object of sensation is the body which moves it through the mediation of the sensory organ, it must be understood that, in so far as we consider such bodies according to the different reasons of their movements, we must necessarily postulate in sensation different powers. For considered in so far as it may be seen, an object is called visible and may not be perceived by any other sense than vision. These objects are in fact of two sorts, for they are either primary, as is the color which we see before anything else, or they are commensurate (or shall we say proportionate), and not color, and inherent in many things that are not colored, such as the fire, the moon, the sun, the stars, and other similar things. Indeed these objects have for this reason no proper name; they are simply called visible, and this includes all those things that are visible through light, such as all the luminous bodies, which are those that I have named above. In so far as an object may be heard, as are the voices and the sounds, it is called audible and may not be perceived by any other sense than hearing. The same might also be said of the other kinds of objects. Such objects are called sensible particulars, since no one of them may be perceived by more than one of the senses which we have named.

---

28 In III, lxvii–lxx, on mode, time, prolation, perfection, imperfection, and the various species and effects of the point or dot.

To be sure, there are certain objects which are called common and which may be perceived by several senses; thus movement, rest, number, shape, and size may manifestly be seen, heard, and touched. Then there are certain other objects which are sensible by accident and which may not be perceived except through the mediation of something else; such are the sonorous bodies, which cannot be heard except through the mediation of the sound which is made in the air, as I have shown in Part II.[e]

The more pleasing and sweet these objects are to their particular sense, the more they are proportioned to it, and vice versa; thus the eye, looking at the sun, is offended, for this object is not proportioned to it. And what the philosophers say is true—that excess in the sensible object, if it does not corrupt the sense, at least corrupts the instrument.[f]

If, then, the particular sensible objects may not be perceived or judged by any other sense than that peculiar to them, as sound is by hearing, as color is by vision, and as the others are in order, let those who strive so hard and take such pains to introduce these intricacies into their compositions tell me (if they will) what and how much pleasure and benefit these may afford to the sense and whether these compositions of theirs are more beautiful and more sonorous than those that do not have such things, which are exclusively visible and fall under no other sense than vision and may not be heard in any way, since they are not common objects, perceptible to several senses, as were those mentioned above. If they have judgment, I know that they will reply that these things afford no benefit at all, for when they have been reduced to simple, ordinary notation and stripped of their ciphers, whatever and however great the harmony heard before, such and as great will be the harmony heard afterward. If, then, they are of no benefit at all in the formation of good harmonies, and if they afford no benefit at all to the sense, why to no purpose multiply the singer's duties and augment his vexations with things of this kind? For when he ought to be intent on singing cheerfully such compositions as are to the purpose, he must stand ready to consider chimeras of this sort, falling (according to the various accidents) under mode, time, and prolation, and he must allow nothing written to pass until he has examined it closely, seeing that if he does otherwise he will be thought (if I may say so) an awkward fellow and an ignoramus. And if these things afford no benefit, as they in truth do not, it seems to me sheer madness that anyone of lofty intelligence should have to end his studies and to waste his time and to vex himself about such irrelevant matters. Thus I counsel everyone to disregard these ciphers

e Chapter 19.   f Aristotle, *De anima*, 424A, 435B.

and to give his attention rather to those things that are productive of good harmonies and sweet ones.

Perhaps someone will say: "Is it not a fine thing to see a tenor well ordered under the signs of mode, time, and prolation, as contrived by the ancient musicians, who gave their attention to almost nothing else?"

It is indeed a fine thing, especially when it is written or painted, and miniatured too, by the hand of an outstanding scribe and miniaturist, using good inks, fine colors, and proportioned measures, and when (as I have seen) there is added to it a coat of arms, a miter, or a cardinal's hat, together with some other splendid object. But of what importance is this if a composition having a tenor written simply and without any intricacy is just as sonorous or as graceless as though it were full of such things?

Thus one may say with truth that this way of composing is simply an unnecessary multiplying of difficulty, and not a multiplying of harmony, and that it affords no benefit at all, since, as the philosophers hold, things are vainly multiplied when there is no purpose. For music, being the science which treats of the sounds and the voices, which are the particular objects of hearing, contemplates only the concord which arises from the strings and the voices (as Ammonius says [g]) and considers nothing else. Thus it seems to me that everything in music that is contemplative without being directed toward this end is vain and useless. For since music was indeed discovered to improve and to delight, as we have said at other times,[h] nothing in music has validity except the voices and the sounds which arise from the strings. These, as Aurelius Cassiodorus imagines, are so named because they move our hearts, a thing he shows most elegantly with the two Latin words *chordae* and *corda*.[i] Thus it is by this path that we perceive the improvement and delight that we derive from hearing harmonies and melodies.

From what has been said we may conclude, then, that this way of composing is not only useless but also harmful, as a loss of time, more precious than anything else, and that the points, lines, circles, semicircles, and other similar things depicted on the page are subject to the sense of vision and not to that of hearing, and that these are matters considered by the geometer, while the sounds and the voices (being in truth the particular objects of hearing) are matters primarily considered by the musician, although he incidentally considers many others.

---

g *In Praedicamentis.*
h I, iii.

i *Variae*, II, xl (Ad Boetium patricium).

Here, perhaps, someone will wish to reprehend and censure me, seeing that many learned and most celebrated ancient musicians, whose fame still lives among us, have practiced this way of composing and that I now wish to censure them.

To this I reply that if these critics will consider the matter, they will find that those compositions that are wrapped round with such restraints afford no greater benefit than they would if they were bare and plain, without any difficulty at all, and they will see that they complain with little reason, and they will understand that they themselves are to be censured, as persons opposed to truth. For although the ancients followed this fashion, they were well aware that such accidents can afford no augmentation or diminution of the harmony. But they practiced such things to show that they were not ignorant of the speculations put forward by certain idle theorists of that day, seeing that the contemplative part of the science then consisted rather in the contemplation of accidents of this sort than in the contemplation of the sounds, the voices, and the other things discussed in Parts I and II of these my labors.

And of this we have the testimony of many books, written by various authors; these treat of nothing but circles and semicircles, with and without points, whole or divided not only once but two and three times, and in them one sees so many points, pauses, colors, ciphers, signs, numbers against numbers, and other strange things that they sometimes appear to be the books of a bewildered merchant. Nor does one read in these books anything that might lead to the understanding of anything subject to the judgment of the sense of hearing, as are the voices and sounds from which the harmonies and melodies arise; they treat only of the things that we have named. And although the fame of some of these musicians still lives honorably among us, they have acquired their reputation, not with such chimeras, but with the good harmonies, the harmonious concentus, and the beautiful inventions which are seen and heard in their works. And although they disordered these with their intricacies, they obliged themselves also, if not through speculation, at least with the aid of practice and their judgment, to reduce their harmonies to the ultimate perfection they could give them, even if the matter was misunderstood and abused by many others, as the many errors committed by the practical musicians in their works bear witness.

Then as to the rational, that is, speculative part, we see that there were few who kept to the good road, for apart from what Boethius wrote in Latin about our science, and this too we find imperfect, there has been no one (leaving Franchino [29] and Faber Stapulensis [30] to one side, for one may say that they were commentators on Boethius) who has gone further in speculating on things pertaining.to music, discovering the true proportions of the musical intervals, except Lodovico Fogliano [31] of Modena,[J] who having perhaps considered what Ptolemy left written on the syntonic diatonic,[32] spared no pains in writing a Latin book on this branch of the science, showing as well as he could the true proportions of the intervals involved. The rest of the theoretical musicians, clinging to what Boethius wrote of these matters, did not wish or were not able to go further and gave themselves over to describing the things that we have named; these they made subject to the quantitative genus, as they called it, under which come mode, time, and prolation, as may be seen in the *Recaneto di musica*,[33] the *Toscanello*,[34] the *Scintille*,[35] and a thousand other similar books.

Besides this there are also conflicting opinions on these questions and long disputations, of which there is no end, then many tracts, invectives, and apologies, written by certain musicians against certain others, in which (although one reads them a thousand times), having read, reread, and examined them, one finds nothing but the innumerable villanies and slanders which they immodestly address to one another (O what shame!) and in the end so little good that one is dumbfounded.

But we may in truth excuse these writers. There were sophists in those days, just as there were sophists in the time of Socrates and Plato, and they were as much esteemed, and this quantitative genus of theirs (one may truly call it an *Arte sofistica* in music and its musicians sophists) was as much practiced in its time as was sophistry in the time of the philosophers in question. Thus we ought continually to praise God and to thank Him that little by little (I know not how) this thing is almost spent and extinct and that He has put us into an age concerned only

---

[J] A note for the malicious. [This note, which does not appear in the earlier editions of the *Istituzioni*, is aimed at Vincenzo Galilei, who in his *Dialogo della musica antica e della moderna* (Florence, 1581), accuses Zarlino of appropriating Fogliano's ideas without giving him credit for them. Zarlino's defense may be seen in his *Sopplimenti*, III, ii.—Ed.]

[29] Zarlino refers here to Franchino Gafori's *Theoricum opus armonice discipline* (Naples, 1480).

[30] *Musica libris quatuor demonstrata* (Paris, 1496).

[31] *Musica theorica* (Venice, 1529); for a summary of Fogliano's contribution see Riemann.

Geschichte der Musiktheorie, 2d ed. (Berlin, 1920), pp. 334-336.

[32] In the syntonic diatonic of Ptolemy, the tetrachords of the Greater Perfect System are divided in the proportions 16:15, 9:8, 10:9. One of Zarlino's principal theses is that this division is the natural and inevitable one and the one actually used in the practical vocal music of his time.

[33] The *Recanetum de musica aurea*, by Stefano Vanneo (Rome, 1533).

[34] The *Toscanello in musica*, by Pietro Aron (Venice, 1523).

[35] The *Scintille, di musica* by G. M. Lanfranco (Brescia, 1533).

with the multiplying of good concentus and good melodies, the true end toward which the musician ought to direct his every work.

·   ·   ·   ·   ·   ·

Book Four

30. HOW THE MODES ARE TO BE JUDGED AND WHAT IS TO BE OBSERVED IN COMPOSING IN THEM

Take note, to begin with, that although we have an almost infinite number of compositions in each of the modes that have been discussed, there are many that are written, not in the simple modes, but in the mixed ones.[36] Thus we find the Fifth Mode mixed with the Twelfth,[37] the Tenth with the First,[38] and so on with the others. An examination of such compositions will make this clear, especially if we examine those of the Fifth Mode that below, instead of the third species of the diapente, E to ♮, have the third of the diatessaron, E to a, and that above, instead of the third species of the diatessaron, ♮ to e, have the second of the diapente, a to e, so that although the species lie within the same diapason, E to e, one of the modes is harmonically divided and maintains the form of the Fifth, while the other is arithmetically divided and maintains the form of the Twelfth. And since the species of the Twelfth Mode are heard repeated over and over again, not only does the greater part of the composition lose all relation to the Fifth Mode, but the whole becomes subject to the Twelfth.

And that this is true will be clear from the following: when we combine these two species, the diatessaron E to a and the diapente a to e, placing the former below and the latter above, we have without a doubt the form of the Twelfth Mode, lying within the third species of the diapason arithmetically divided; thus a composition that we judge to be of the Fifth Mode comes to have nothing by which we might judge that it is of the Fifth unless it is its ending on E, which is a most deceptive thing. For although some would have us judge a composition by its final (as by its end and not by what precedes it), seeing that everything is rightly judged by or in its end, it does not follow from this that we may come to recognize the mode on which a composition is based by this alone. Thus we ought to believe, not that we may judge by this alone, but that we must wait until the composition has reached its end and there

---

36 In IV, xiv, Zarlino defines a mixed mode as one in which a fifth or fourth belonging to another mode is heard often repeated.

37 Glarean's Phrygian and Hypoaeolian.

38 Glarean's Hypomixolydian and Ionian.

judge it rightly, that is, by its form, for the composition is then complete and has its form, which is the occasion of our judgment. Note, however, that this has two occasions: one is the form of the composition as a whole; the other is its end, that is, its final. But since form is that which gives being to a thing, it seems reasonable to me that our judgment should be based on the form of the whole and not, as some have wished, on the final alone.

And if a composition is to be judged from its form, that is, from its procedure, as is the obligation, it is not inconsistent that, rejecting the final, a principal mode may conclude on the central step of its diapason, harmonically divided, and in a similar way a collateral mode at either extreme of its diapason, arithmetically divided. How elegantly this can be done may be seen in the motet "Si bona suscepimus," composed for five voices by Verdelot,[39] and in the madrigal "O invidia nemica di virtute," likewise composed to be sung with five voices by Adriano; [40] although these have from beginning to end the procedure of the Eleventh Mode in the one case and of the Fourth in the other, they conclude, not on their true finals, but on their central steps.[41]

And what I say of the Fifth and Twelfth Modes is also true of the others which, for brevity's sake, I omit. Thus we should not be astonished if we often hear no difference between a composition ending on E and one ending on a, for they are written in mixed modes in the manner we have described; if they were composed in the simple ones there is no doubt that we would hear a great difference in harmony between them.

Thus in judging any composition, whatever it may be, we have to consider it most carefully from beginning to end and to determine the form in which it is written, whether in that of the First, or of the Second, or of some other mode, having an eye to the cadences, which throw a great light on this question; then we may judge it even though it concludes, not on its proper final, but on its central step or on some other that may prove to the purpose.

Nor is it inconsistent that we use this way of ending in our compositions, seeing that the ecclesiastics have used it also in their chants. This may be seen at the end of the Kyrie eleison called "For semidoubles" or "Of the apostles"; [42] although this clearly has the form of the Third Mode, it ends on a, the confinal, as they call it, and the central step of

39 *Motetti del fiore a 5*, II (Lyons, 1532), No. 18; reprinted by Maldeghem in his *Trésor musical, Musique religieuse*, 1892, pp. 8 ff.
40 *Musica nova di Adriano Willaert* (Venice, 1559), No. 24.

41 In other words, the motet by Verdelot is Aeolian, not Phrygian, while the madrigal by Willaert is Hypodorian, not Aeolian.
42 *Grad. Rom.*, p. 15*. (Cunctipotens Genitor Deus).

the diapason D to d within which the form of this mode lies. Then there is the offertory "Domine fac mecum," [43] from the mass for the Wednesday after the third Sunday in Lent, which lies between the extremes F and e; besides this there are two other chants: one is "Tollite hostias," [44] sung after the communion of the mass for the eighteenth Sunday after Pentecost, which lies between the extremes just mentioned; the other is "Per signum crucis," [45] sung on the solemn feasts of the Finding and Exaltation of the Holy Cross, which lies between the extremes F and g. These chants have the form of the Ninth Mode, for they contain the modulation of its diapente, G to d, and of its diatessaron, d to g; they conclude on ♮, the central step of the diapente. It is quite true that in the opinion of certain moderns [46] they are to be attributed to the Fourteenth, but I leave this to the judgment of anyone of intelligence. In some of the modern books these chants are found transposed, without ♭, from their natural position to the diapente below, either through the ignorance or carelessness of the copyists or through the arrogance of persons of little understanding. But in the good and correct copies, of which I have beside me an old one, written by hand, which may still be seen and examined, they lie between the extremes named above.

Note that what I call the form of the mode is the octave divided into its fifth and fourth, and that these two parts, arising from harmonic or arithmetic division, are heard repeated many times in their proper modes. Thus, when we compose, we may know what is to guide us in leading the parts of our composition and in putting the cadences at places suitable for the distinction of the words; as has been said, it is the mode. And in a similar way we may know how to proceed in judging a composition of any kind, whether plainsong or figured music.

. . . . .

32. HOW THE HARMONIES ARE ADAPTED TO THE WORDS
PLACED BENEATH THEM

Seeing that the time and place require it, it now remains to be determined how one ought to combine the harmonies with the words placed beneath them. I say "to combine the harmonies with the words" for this reason: although (following Plato's opinion) we have said in

43 *Ibid.*, pp. 133–134.
44 *Ibid.*, pp. 374–375.
45 *Ibid.*, p. 492.
46 Namely Glarean (*Dodecachordon*, II, xxv,

III, xxi; Bohn's translation, pp. 101–102, 303–305), from whom Zarlino borrows all the examples of this paragraph.

Part II [47] that melody is a combination of speech, harmony, and rhythm,[k] and although it seems that in such a combination no one of these things is prior to another, Plato gives speech the first place and makes the other two parts subservient to it, for after he has shown the whole by means of the parts, he says that harmony and rhythm ought to follow speech. And this is the obligation. For if in speech, whether by way of narrative or of imitation (and these occur in speech), matters may be treated that are joyful or mournful, and grave or without gravity, and again modest or lascivious, we must also make a choice of a harmony and a rhythm similar to the nature of the matters contained in the speech in order that from the combination of these things, put together with proportion, may result a melody suited to the purpose.

We ought indeed to listen to what Horace says in his epistle on the *Art of Poetry:*

Versibus exponi tragicis res comica non volt; [48]

and to what Ovid says in this connection:

Callimachi numeris non est dicendus Achilles;
Cydippe non est oris, Homere, tui.[l]

For if the poet is not permitted to write a comedy in tragic verse, the musician will also not be permitted to combine unsuitably these two things, namely, harmony and words.[49] Thus it will be inappropriate if in a joyful matter he uses a mournful harmony and a grave rhythm, nor where funereal and tearful matters are treated is he permitted to use a joyful harmony and a rhythm that is light or rapid, call it as we will. On the contrary, he must use joyful harmonies and rapid rhythms in joyful matters, and in mournful ones, mournful harmonies and grave rhythms, so that everything may be done with proportion.

He who has studied what I have written in Part III and has considered the nature of the mode in which he wishes to write his composition will, I think, know precisely how to do this. In so far as he can, he must take

---

k *Republic,* III. [*S.R.* I, 4. Ambros. in his *Geschichte der Musik,* III, 3d ed. (Leipzig, 1893), 163, calls attention to an earlier sixteenth-century reference to this passage in the foreword by Johannes Ott to the *Missae tredecim* (Nuremberg, 1539): "Thus we see that learned musicians have diligently followed the rule that, in Plato, Socrates lays down for melodies: that the musician ought to make the melody follow the words, and not the words the melody. For since the greatest gravity resides in these words of the church, the composers clothe the musical sounds with a becoming gravity."—Ed.]

l *Remediorum amoris,* 381-382. ["Achilles must not be told of in the numbers of Callimachus; Cydippe suits not thy utterance, Homer." —Mozley]

47 Chapter 12.
48 Line 89. "A theme for Comedy refuses to be set forth in the verses of Tragedy." [Fairclough]
49 The "Rules to be observed in dittying" given by Morley on pages 177 and 178 of his *Plain and Easy Introduction* (London, 1597) are in effect an abridged translation of the remainder of this chapter.

care to accompany each word in such a way that, if it denotes harshness, hardness, cruelty, bitterness, and other things of this sort, the harmony will be similar, that is, somewhat hard and harsh, but so that it does not offend. In the same way, if any word expresses complaint, grief, affliction, sighs, tears, and other things of this sort, the harmony will be full of sadness.[m]

Wishing to express effects of the first sort, he will do best to accustom himself to arrange the parts of his composition so that they proceed with such movements as are without the semitone, as are those of the tone and ditone, allowing the major sixth or thirteenth, which are naturally somewhat harsh, to be heard above the lowest tone of the concentus, and accompanying these with the syncope of the fourth or eleventh above this same tone, using rather slow movements; with these he may use the syncope of the seventh. But wishing to express effects of the second sort, he will use (always observing the rules that have been given) such movements as proceed by the semitone or semiditone or in some other similar way, often taking above the lowest tone of his composition the minor sixth or thirteenth, which are naturally soft and sweet, especially when they are combined in the right ways and with discretion and judgment.

Note, however, that the expression of these effects is to be attributed not only to the consonances that we have named, used as we have directed, but also to the movements that the parts make in singing, which are of two sorts—natural and accidental. The natural movements are those made between the natural steps of the music, where no sign or accidental step intervenes, and these have more virility than those made by means of the accidental steps, marked with the signs ♯ and ♭, which are indeed accidental and somewhat languid. In the same way there arises from the accidental movements a sort of interval called accidental, while from the natural movements arise the intervals called natural. We ought then to bear in mind that the natural movements make the music somewhat more sonorous and virile, while the accidental ones make it softer and somewhat more languid. Thus the natural movements may serve to express effects of our first sort, and the accidental ones may serve for the rest, so that combining with some judgment the intervals of the major and minor consonances and the natural and accidental movements, we will succeed in imitating the words with a thoroughly suitable harmony.

---

m Even though this be censured by some of our modern Aristarchs. [Namely, Vincenzo Galilei. See pages 88 and 89 of his *Dialogo della musica antica e della moderna* (pp. 125–126 below).—Ed.] But as to this, see Chapter 11 of Book VIII of our *Supplements*.

Then as to the observance of the rhythms, the primary consideration is the matter contained in the words: if this is joyful, we ought to proceed with swift and vigorous movements, that is, with figures carrying swiftness, such as the minim and semiminim; if it is mournful, we ought to proceed with slow and lingering movements.

Thus Adriano has taught us to express the one sort and the other in many compositions, among them "I vidi in terra angelici costumi," "Aspro core e selvaggio," and "Ove ch'i posi gli occhi," all written for six voices, "Quando fra l'altre donne" and "Giunto m'ha Amor" for five voices,[50] and innumerable others.

And although the ancients understood rhythms in another way than the moderns do, as is clear from many passages in Plato, we ought not only to keep this consideration in mind but also to take care that we adapt the words of the speech to the musical figures in such a way and with such rhythms that nothing barbarous is heard, not making short syllables long and long syllables short as is done every day in innumerable compositions, a truly shameful thing.[n] Nor do we find this vice only in figured music but, as is obvious to every man of judgment, in plainsong also, for there are few chants that are not filled with barbarous things of this kind. Thus over and over again we hear length given to the penultimate syllables of such words as *Dominus, Angélus, Filius, miracúlum, gloría,* and many others, syllables which are properly short and fleeting. To correct this would be a most praiseworthy undertaking and an easy one, for by changing it a very little, one would make the chant most suitable, nor would this change its original form, since this consists solely of many figures or notes in ligature, placed under the short syllables in question and inappropriately making them long when a single figure would suffice.

In a similar way we ought to take care not to separate the parts of the speech from one another with rests, so long as a clause, or any part of it, is incomplete and the sense of the words imperfect, a thing done by some of little intelligence, and unless a period is complete and the sense of the words perfect we ought not to make a cadence, especially one of the principal ones, or to use a rest larger than that of the minim, nor should the rest of the minim be used within the intermediate points. For this is in truth a vicious thing, and for all that it is practiced by some little re-

n But as to this, what has been said in Chapter 13 of Book VIII of our *Supplements* [On the three sorts of accents: grammatical, rhetorical, and musical.—Ed.] ought by all means to be carefully considered, so that all may go well and no error be committed.

50 *Musica nova di Adriano Willaert* (Venice, 1559), nos. 38, 33, 39, 26, and 30.

pentent practical musicians of our time, anyone inclined to heed the matter
may easily observe and understand it.

Thus, since the matter is of great importance, the composer ought to
open his eyes and not keep them closed so that he may not be thought
ignorant of a thing so necessary, and he ought to take care to use the rest
of the minim or semiminim (whichever suits his purpose) at the head of
the intermediate points of the speech, for these have the force of commas,
while at the head of the periods he may use whatever quantity of rest
he chooses, for it seems to me that when the rests are used in this manner
one may best distinguish the members of the period from one another
and without any difficulty hear the perfect sense of the words.

33. THE PROCEDURE TO BE FOLLOWED IN PLACING THE MUSICAL FIGURES UNDER THE WORDS

Who will ever be able to recite, unless with great difficulty, the disorder
and the inelegance that many practical musicians support and have supported and the confusion that they have caused in suitably adapting the
musical figures to the words of the speech? When I reflect that a science
that has brought law and good order to other things is in this respect so
disorderly that it is barely tolerable, I cannot help complaining, for some
compositions are indeed dumbfounding to hear and to see. It is not only
that in the declamation of the words one hears confused periods, incomplete clauses, unsuitable cadences, singing without order, innumerable
errors in applying the harmonies to the words, little regard for mode,
badly accommodated parts, passages without beauty, rhythms without
proportion, movements without purpose, figures badly numbered in time
and prolation, and a thousand other disorders; one also finds the musical
figures so adapted to the words that the singer cannot determine or discover a suitable way of performing them. Now he sees two syllables under many figures, now under two figures many syllables. Now he hears
the singer of another part who, at some point where the words require
it, uses the apostrophe or elides the vowels; wishing to do the same in
his part, he succeeds in missing the beautiful and elegant manner of singing and in putting a figure that carries length under a short syllable, or
vice versa. Now he hears the singers of the other parts make a syllable
long which in his must necessarily be short. Thus, hearing all this diversity, he does not know what to do and remains thoroughly bewildered
and confused.

And since the whole consists in adapting the musical figures to the words beneath them, and since in composition it is required that the musical figures be used to mark and note the pitches so that the sounds and the voices may be properly performed in every modulation; and seeing that it is by means of such figures that we perform the rhythm, that is, the length and brevity of the syllables of the speech, and that over these syllables there are often put, not one, two, or three, but even more such figures, as may be required by the accents suitably arranged in the speech; therefore, in order that no confusion may arise in adapting the figures to the syllables and to the words, and wishing (if I can) to end all this disorder; to the many rules I have already given in various places in accordance with the requirements of my materials, I now add these, which will serve both the composer and the singer and will at the same time be to my purpose.

1. A suitable figure is to be placed below each long or short syllable so that nothing barbarous will be heard. For in figured music each musical figure that stands alone and is not in ligature (apart from the semiminim and all those that are smaller than the semiminim) carries its own syllable with it. This rule is observed in plainsong also, for to each square figure is adapted a syllable of its own, excepting for the middle notes, which are sometimes treated like minims or even semiminims, as may be seen in many chants, especially in the chant for the Nicene Creed, "Credo in unum Deum," which they call the Credo cardinale.[51]

2. Not more than one syllable, and that at the beginning, is to be adapted to each ligature of several notes or figures, whether in figured music or in plainsong.

3. No syllable is to be adapted to the dot placed after the figures of figured music, although this is sung.

4. It is not usual to place a syllable below a semiminim, or below those figures that are smaller than the semiminim, or below the figure immediately following.

5. It is not customary to place any syllable below the figures immediately following a dotted semibreve or dotted minim, when these following figures are valued at less than the dots, as are semiminims after a dotted semibreve or chromas after a dotted minim; the same is true of the figures that immediately follow these.

6. Should it be necessary to place a syllable below a semiminim, one may also place another syllable below the figure following.

7. At the beginning of a composition, or after any rest in the middle, the first figure, whatever it may be, must necessarily carry with it a syllable.

8. In plainsong no word or syllable is ever repeated, although one some-

times hears this done, a thing indeed to be censured; in figured music such repetitions are sometimes tolerated—not of a syllable or of a word, but of some part of the speech whose sense is complete. This may be done when there are figures in such quantity that words may be repeated conveniently. But to repeat a thing many times over does not, in my opinion, go over well, unless it be done to give greater emphasis to words that have in them some grave sense and are worthy of consideration.

9. When all the syllables of a period or of one part of the speech have been adapted to the musical figures and there remain only the penultimate syllable and the last, the penultimate syllable will have the privilege of bearing a number of small figures—two, three, or some other quantity—provided, however, that it be long and not short, for if it were short a barbarism would occur. Singing in this way, there arises what many call a *neuma*, which occurs when many figures are sung above a single syllable. But when figures are placed in this way, they offend against our first rule.

10. The final syllable of the speech will fall below the final figure of the composition, if our rules are observed.

Seeing that the reader will find innumerable examples of all these things if he will examine the learned works of Adriano and of those who have been and are his disciples and observers of the good rules, I shall go on without giving further examples to the discussion of the ligatures formed from certain of the musical figures, for these are useful in this connection.

7. Pietro Cerone

An Italian writer for Spanish readers, Pietro Cerone was born in Bergamo, probably in the 1560's; in 1592 he visited Spain, where he later became a musician of the royal chapel, serving under Philip II and, after 1598, under his successor, Philip III. By 1609 he had returned to Italy; in this year he published a little treatise on plainsong in which he described himself as a musician of the royal chapel in Naples and informed his readers that a more extensive work of his, *El melopeo y maestro*, was about to appear. The book was not actually published until 1613.

El melopeo, which runs to 22 "books," 849 chapters, and 1,160 pages, is an undigested and often indigestible mass of information and misinformation about music, some of it useful, much of it useless. For its time it is distinctly conservative, even old-fashioned: it shows little understanding for Marenzio, and the names of Monteverdi and· Marco da Gagliano are not so much as mentioned. Its tasteless pedantry was ridiculed with devastating effect by the eighteenth-century critic Antonio Eximeno, who called it "a musical monster" and, in his satiric novel *Don Lazarillo Vizcardi* (1802), treated it much as Cervantes had treated the romances of chivalry. Other critics have commended it for its sound musicianship, its admirable choice of examples, and its enlightening observations, such as those on the nature and meaning of the two- and three-part interludes of the sixteenth-century Mass and Magnificat, translated below. Neither verdict tells the whole story. The book is uneven and requires a discriminating reader; it has grave defects, but it also has redeeming merits.

From El melopeo y maestro [1]
[*1613*]

Book XII

12. THE MANNER TO BE OBSERVED IN COMPOSING A MOTET

You HAVE seen how many directions and how many considerations the contrapuntist, and still more the composer, must observe, both as regards the correct manner of singing and the greater convenience and ease of the singer and as regards what is proper to the workmanship. To be sure, one can neither give nor enumerate exactly all the directions which commonly occur in compositions. But those that I have mentioned are at least of such a nature and number that an elaborate composition may be written with fewer errors and fewer faults than some of those that one hears sung today in churches and in musical exercises. Apart from the aforesaid general directions I shall now give particular ones which will serve to order any kind of composition whatever in accordance with its proper style and in conformity with the true manner and with what has been observed by famous musicians.

When he wishes to write a motet, then, the composer must see to it that the voices sing with continual gravity and majesty, particularly the bass part, preserving this order in the parts from beginning to end, even though we see it disregarded in these times, particularly by those of my nation. These musicians dispose the lively parts and divisions in such a way that their compositions seem to be madrigals and sometimes canzonets; instead of the syncopated semibreve, they use the syncopated minim, suited neither to the gravity of the motet nor to its majesty; what is more, they use the semiminim rest and even the quaver rest, not only once, but continuing to the very end, a thing you will not find observed by those good ecclesiastical composers and excellent musicians Josquin, Phinot, Adriano,[2] Morales, Palestrina, Guerrero, Victoria, etc. And since the gravity which I say that motets must maintain might be so slow and heavy and broad that it would be unsuitable, unless for the Gloria Patri of the Magnificat, the "Et incarnatus est" of the Mass, the Lamentations

---

1 Text: The original edition (Naples, 1613),   2 Willaert.
pp. 685–691.

of Holy Week, or the Adoration of the Most Holy Sacrament of the Eucharist, I shall now set down here a few particular directions to be observed in composing a motet with the gravity and majesty of which I have spoken.

1. Let the gravity in motets be maintained in this manner: when several parts are singing and a breve occurs in one of them, let the other parts proceed with minims, or with semiminims, or with semibreves placed on the arsis of the measure, or with a dotted minim, also on the arsis, which is the better position; failing this, let them be on the thesis.

2. Because of their great rapidity and liveliness, quavers and semiquavers are out of place here; too many semibreves are also out of place if all the parts continually run about in notes of this denomination above the aforesaid breve or semibreve on the arsis of the measure.

3. If the composition is for four or five voices (when all the parts are singing), let two or three parts sustain throughout one measure (when singing in the smaller measure) [3] or throughout several measures while the others proceed with minims and semiminims, but not with quavers and still less with semiquavers, and this (as I have said) in order not to fall into the style of madrigals or of secular chansons. And in this way the workmanship will have gravity and will preserve the true motet style.

4. Note that the aforesaid breve or semibreve should not always be placed in one and the same part (for thus it would come to form a plainsong), but now in one, now in another, the parts proceeding always with different motions and unequal values, provided the words do not demand that they be combined with gravity and majesty and with large and equal values, as we see sometimes in the works of excellent composers.

5. The invention of the motet should be newly invented, although many have composed motets upon the matter or principal motives of a madrigal, chanson, or *tiento*, a thing not wholly pleasing to me for the reasons given in Chapter 69 of Book 1 on page 198,[4] and because the workmanship in motets should be new throughout and in all respects, and also because such an order is permitted only in masses.

6. When the motet is divided into two sections and the closing words of the second section are the same as those of the first, the composer (if he wishes) may in a similar way repeat in the second section the same music that was sung in the first, a thing that as a rule occurs when the words are taken from the Responds and their Verses.[5]

---

3 See p. 80 below, where the "smaller" measure is identified with "common" time, the "larger" with "alla breve."

4 That we ought to employ music in spiritual matters and not in profane ones.

5 When the words of a motet are those of a Respond and its Verse, the "prima pars" is regularly a setting of the Respond; in the "secunda pars" the setting of the Verse is normally followed by a return of the concluding line or lines

7. But it is true that, if the first section closes with an inconclusive cadence, the second should conclude, not with this final, but with the final of the tone in order to preserve the above-mentioned order of final cadences. The same license is used also in a motet in one section as often as it takes the same words, which is nearly always in the middle of the motet.[6]

8. The motet must close on the final of the tone in which it is composed in order that one may easily recognize what tone it is in. If it is divided into two sections, it is true that the first (if the composer wishes) may close with an inconclusive final, namely, on the step which bounds the diapente of the tone, provided the second section always closes with the final cadence proper to the tone.

9. And note that, if the motet is divided into three, four, or more sections, the composer must not fail to end the first and last sections on the true final, the other sections remaining at his pleasure.

10. But provided he does not make two inconclusive cadences in succession on the confinal of the tone.

Let these particular directions suffice for composing a motet with its necessary parts, never departing from the other rules and directions.

13. THE MANNER TO BE OBSERVED IN COMPOSING A MASS

The manner, or style, to be observed in composing a mass agrees with that of the motet as regards the slow movement which the parts should maintain, but not as regards the order, which is very different.

1. In the motet, the beginnings of the first, second, and following sections differ from one another, and the invention, provided it is appropriate to the mode, conforms to the composer's pleasure and fancy. But in composing a mass, it is perforce necessary and obligatory that the inventions at the beginnings of the first Kyrie, the Gloria, the Credo, the Sanctus, and the Agnus Dei should be one and the same; one and the same in invention, that is, but not in consonances and accompaniments. In other words, if the beginning of the invention of the first Kyrie runs *Ut re fa fa mi re*, the treble entering first, then the alto, then the tenor, and finally the bass, then not only the Gloria, but also the Credo, the Sanctus, and the Agnus Dei should begin with the same invention, namely, *Ut re fa fa mi re*, yet with different consonances and in different

---

of the Respond, usually in the same setting as before. For a conveniently accessible example of this very common procedure, see the motet "Ecce quomodo moritur justus," by Jacob Gallus, in Schering, *Geschichte der Musik in Beispielen* (Leipzig, 1931), No. 131.

6 See for example Palestrina's motets "Aegypte noli flere" and "Surge Petre," *Collected Works*, IV, 121 and 130.

manners. For example, if the treble began the imitation in the first Kyrie, let another voice (the tenor, alto, or bass) begin it in the Gloria, another in the Credo, another in the Sanctus, and still another in the Agnus Dei. And should it happen that the treble or some other part begins two or three times, take care that the other parts enter each time with consonances other than those with which they entered before. Thus all the aforesaid beginnings should maintain variety in the parts and consonances, but not in the invention or subject.

2. When the first Kyrie is finished, the Christe may be written upon some subsidiary motive from the same motet or madrigal (whichever it is) from which the principal subject was borrowed. Know also that the composer may here use some invention of his own, provided it is appropriate to the tone and not in another manner.

3. The beginnings of the last Kyrie and of the second and third Agnus Dei are in every respect at the composer's pleasure. Nevertheless, there is nothing to forbid his borrowing some other subsidiary motive from the motet or madrigal upon which the mass is composed.

4. The endings of the last Kyrie, the Gloria, the Credo, the Sanctus, the Osanna (for the Sanctus is always divided, for greater solemnity, into three or four sections), and the third Agnus Dei should perforce be in imitation, following the invention of the motet or madrigal upon which the mass is composed, preserving in each case the order which I have said should be preserved in the beginnings and imitations, namely, that all these endings should be the same in invention and termination, yet accompanied with different consonances and in different manners.

5. But the endings of the Christe, the Et in terra, the Patrem omnipotentem (dividing the Gloria and Credo into several sections), the Pleni sunt coeli or Benedictus (beginning or ending the section), and the second Agnus Dei may close on the confinal of the tone, provided two endings in succession do not close on the confinal, although they may do so on the final or principal.

6. In the course of the mass, the more use one makes (whether with or without imitation) of motives from the middle or inside of the composition upon which the mass is written, the better and the more praiseworthy the work will be.

7. When the mass is not ferial, or for week days, the Kyries, the Sanctus (with all that follows) and the Agnus Dei's should be solemnly ordered, repeating several times the motives of the imitation or invention of the subject; when it is ferial and without solemnity, it suffices to

use the invention two or three times at most, always closing with it, that is, without introducing new inventions or other matter.

8. The Gloria and Credo (provided they do not contain some duo or trio, which should be solemn, imitated, and ordered with much artifice) are composed as continuous movements, without solemnity and with less imitation of the parts, using imitations that are short, clear, familiar, and closely woven, unlike those of the Kyries, the Sanctus, and the Agnus Dei's, which (as I have said) should be long, elaborate, less familiar, and less closely woven.

9. It may be seen that good composers have taken care to make the parts sing all together, using such slow notes as the breve, semibreve, and minim, with devout consonances and with harmonious intervals, upon the words "Jesu Christe." This is done because of the reverence and decorum due to their meanings. The same is usually observed upon the words "Et incarnatus est" to "Crucifixus." To use imitations and lively progressions here, with other graces, is a very great error and a sign of great ignorance.

10. The composer (ending the section) is at liberty to write the Christe, the Crucifixus, the Pleni sunt coeli, the Benedictus, and the second Agnus Dei for fewer voices than are used in the work as a whole. In other words, if the mass is for five voices, the aforesaid sections may be written for four or for three; if the mass is for four voices, they may be written for three or even two. But it should be noted that, being written for fewer voices, these sections should be composed with greater artifice and greater learning and in a more lofty and more elegant style. These reduced parts are the flower of the whole work, so made in imitation of the perfect writer of comedy; [7] assuming that in the course of a comedy he uses verses of great elegance, learning, and savor, all leading up to the detail that a character recites some sonnet or madrigal, who does not know that this sonnet or madrigal is woven with greater artifice, elegance, and grace than all the rest of the comedy? A similar procedure is followed by learned and excellent composers in the duos and trios which they interpolate among the movements of their works.

11. And to conclude their work with greater harmony and greater sonority, composers usually write the last Agnus Dei for more voices, adding one or two parts to the regular parts of the composition, doubling as they find most convenient whichever part they please.

---

[7] Possibly a reference to Lope de Vega, who gives rules for the construction of these lyric in-terpolations in his *Arte nuevo de hacer comedias* (1609).

12. As a rule, the mass is usually composed upon some motet, madrigal, or chanson (as I have said), even though by another author; thus it afterwards takes its title from the first words with which the said motet, madrigal, or chanson, begins, thus "Missa Virtute magna," [8] "Missa Vestiva i colli," [9] "Missa En espoir." [10] If the composer does not wish to use the above-mentioned materials, but prefers to write his mass upon a new invention of his own, he may give it a title of another sort, thus "Missa sine nomine," or, if it is short, he may call it "Missa brevis" or "Missa L'hora è tarda." He may also name it from the subject of the composition, as was done by Pietro Ponzio, Pietro Vinci, and Morales, who, having contrived masses dependent upon the notes of the hexachord, gave them the title "Missa Ut re mi fa sol la"; others have used "Missa super voces musicales"; [11] and Josquin took for a subject or theme the five notes *La sol fa re mi*. [12] If the mass is composed upon the formulas of any tone it should take its title from the name of the tone to which the formulas belong, thus "Missa Primi toni," "Missa Secundi toni," etc. If it is written upon a plainsong, that is, if it is formed upon the notes of the Kyries, Glorias, Credos, Sanctuses, Agnus Dei's, or any other chant, but using the various figures of figured music, it should be named after the plainsong, namely, "Missa de Beata Virgine," "Missa Apostolorum," "Missa Dominicalis," "Missa Ecce sacerdos magnus," "Missa Ad coenam Agni providi." [13]

Take care always to observe the above-mentioned order in the beginnings, middle parts, and endings of the principal movements of the mass; failing this, know of a certainty that you will not be preserving the true order of composing masses which to this day we see used by the best composers and most excellent musicians.

Masses composed for several choruses should be written with short imitations, plain consonances, and less artifice.

---

[8] Masses on the motet "Virtute magna," by Mathieu Lasson, were written by Clemens non papa and Palestrina.

[9] Masses on Palestrina's madrigal "Vestiva i colli" were written by Palestrina himself and by a number of other composers, among them G. M. Nanino, Ruggiero Giovannelli, Giulio Belli, Felice Anerio, G. B. Cesena, Johannes Nucius, and Rudolf Lassus (see H. J. Moser, "Vestiva i colli," *Archiv für Musikforschung*, IV (1939), 129–156.

[10] A mass on Gombert's chanson "En espoir" was written by Clemens non papa.

[11] Other masses on the hexachord or *voces musicales* were written by Brumel, de Kerle, Palestrina, and Soriano.

[12] *Werken, Missen*, I (Amsterdam, 1926), 35–36.

[13] Masses on "Ecce sacerdos magnus" and "Ad coenam Agni providi" were included by Palestrina in his First Book of Masses (1554); there is another mass on "Ad coenam Agni providi" by Animuccia (1567).

14. THE MANNER TO BE OBSERVED IN COMPOSING PSALMS

Although in these kingdoms of Spain the singing of psalms in figured music is not customary, except in falso bordone, I do not wish to omit an explanation of what must be observed in writing them for the benefit of those who care to do so.

In composing psalms, even to omit imitating the psalmody will be no error, for if one were to imitate the plainsong in all the parts, repeating the motives, the verse would be very long, very elaborate, and overly solemn, solemnity being unsuited to psalmody. Yet there are Italians who have written psalms with more solemnity and with more art than they use in writing Magnificats, which is on due consideration a great error. But an imitation may very well be made in two parts, or even in one, in order that the mode may be more easily recognized, and if all the parts begin together, such a beginning will be equally free from blame.

Further, it is necessary to pattern the mediation of the figured music on the cadence of the mediation of the plainsong, in order that it may be immediately recognized as psalmody and also because the ancients (whose observations and precepts we are obliged to follow) always took care to do this, especially because these mediations are so necessary to distinguish this kind of composition from others. The final cadence should vary in conformity with the differences of the Euouae or Seculorum Amen.

Be it further observed that the music should be such as does not obscure the words, which should be very distinct and clear, so that all the parts will seem to enunciate together, no more, no less, as in a falso bordone, without long or elegant passages or any novelty other than ordinary consonances, introducing from time to time some short and commonplace imitation, following the practice we see observed by the choral composers, particularly by the Reverend Dom Matteo Asola and by the Reverend Dom Pietro Ponzio.[14]

Many composers (as I have said) have written psalms with much artifice, very finished and solemn, which, lacking the elements that I have mentioned, are considered good and learned as regards music, but neither good nor appropriate as regards psalmody; instead of being short, they were long; instead of using ordinary consonances, they used farfetched and unauthorized passages; instead of setting the words clearly, they set them in a very obscure and cumbrous style; instead of making

---

14 For examples of the psalmodic style of Asola and Ponzio see Torchi, *L'arte musicale in* *Italia*, II, 373, and Burney, *A General History of Music*, III, 171.

them plain, they made them solemn and more imitated, repeating the imitations several times and continuing the plainsong in all the parts, which is the distinctive and particular style of the Magnificat.

It is true that, if the composer wishes, he may write the Gloria Patri in a more learned style, letting the plainsong continue in all the parts, adding one or two voices to those he had. In other words, if the other verses are for four voices, he may let the Gloria be for five or more. This may also be written in canon, but the whole should be succinctly ordered, leaving greater solemnity and greater artifice to the Gloria of the Magnificat and of the other canticles.

To conclude, I say that any invention used in the verses of the psalms should be very short, formed of few notes and these of small value, and also that the parts should enter in succession after rests of not more than one, two, three, or sometimes four measures. And this should be observed both to avoid making the verses long and to avoid falling into the style of the three privileged canticles.

Other particular directions and rules are given in Book 16, in treating of the tones of figured music.

15. THE MANNER TO BE OBSERVED IN COMPOSING THE THREE PRINCIPAL CANTICLES [15]

As is the custom, the three principal canticles, namely, the Magnificat, the Nunc dimittis, and the Benedictus Dominus Deus Israel, are always made solemn; for this reason, they must be composed in a more lofty style and with more art and more skill than the other canticles and the psalms. To this end the following order is observed.

In the first place, all the voices paraphrase the plainsong in imitation (although they sometimes sing some other imitation discovered by the composer), and these imitations should always be differently ordered. Herein lies the chief difficulty, for while the plainsong is always the same, the figured music must be ordered in different ways.

The parts may begin in succession after one, two, three, or four breve rests (the composition being in the larger or alla breve measure) or after the same number of semibreve rests (the composition being in the smaller or common measure), and this order should be strictly observed, at least by the first part, which should enter after a rest of not more than two measures; the other rests, coming later, are not observed with

---

[15] The three gospel-canticles Magnificat, Benedictus, and Nunc dimittis outrank the Old Testament canticles and psalms, and occupy fixed positions at Vespers, Lauds, and Compline.

the same rigor, for the remaining parts often rest beyond their prescribed limits, being unable to enter easily with the imitation. The same practice, I may say, is observed in beginning motets and the principal sections of the mass.

Take care to let one of the parts (the tenor is the most appropriate) sing the mediation of the plainsong with its proper cadence and the ending with its final cadence in accordance with the difference of the Seculorum which the composer has chosen.

1. Composers usually let all the parts imitate the intonation of the solemn plainsong [16] at the beginning of the verses, always varying the imitation and using different manners; this is the best plan.

2. It is also usual that, while two parts sing the intonation, the other parts sing some free and arbitrary invention, as may be seen in the Magnificat in the first tone by Morales, namely at "Anima mea Dominum." [17]

3. Sometimes, however, one lets all the parts sing certain inventions appropriate to the tone, disregarding the intonation of the plainsong, and it is the usual custom to pattern the end of the verse on the ending of the plainsong (at least in one part) in order that it may not end without giving to the canticle the solemnity of the ecclesiastical music, with its gravity and authority, and in order that it may be recognized for what it is.

4. There is also another very good order, often observed by good composers: one part sings the entire plainsong from beginning to end, interpolating rests from time to time, and upon this the other parts go on to sing various inventions, preserving always the gravity and the artifice belonging to the canticles and altogether disregarding the style of choral counterpoint, disregarding it, that is, without making the parts run about too much with consecutive minims and semiminims.

5. One may also let one part sing the plainsong up to the mediation of the verse, concluding it with its proper cadence; after this, all the parts sing in new manners to the end without imitating the plainsong at all, except to close on the final of the mode in accordance with the position of the Seculorum.

6. The opposite of this is also possible: after having reached the mediation of the verse without imitating the plainsong either more or less than this, one or two parts sing the ending of the plainsong.

---

16 That is, the gospel-canticle tone.
17 The procedure is equally well illustrated by the corresponding passage in Palestrina's Magnificat in Tone II, *Complete Works,* xxvii, 6.

Pedrell has published a Magnificat in Tone VIII by Morales in *Hispaniae schola musica sacra,* I, 20–23.

7. Another manner used is this: one part sings half the plainsong and another part finishes the remainder.

8. There is no doubt that Magnificats may also be written (as certain persons often write them today) without obligation either to plainsong or to inventions; these, however, will be taken by those expert in the musical profession for what they are, namely for things improperly and injudiciously written. This is because the composing of canticles in the manner of psalms is permitted for special use, on simple feasts and ferial days, in the services of those churches where figured music is sung every day, for although the text is privileged, the day does not require solemnity.

For greater decorum and gravity, the Gloria Patri is written with many breves and semibreves, interpolating occasional dissonances, and with all the parts singing continuously in order that the conclusion may be more full and sonorous. Thus it is unsuitable to end in fewer parts than were used in the composition as a whole, with two or three voices singing, as is done in other verses, except that, for the convenience of the music and of the composer, a rest of three or four measures is permitted. It may also be ordered in canon, adding one or more voices, as I have said of the Gloria Patri of the psalms; the same is true of the "Sicut erat," composed upon the even-numbered verses, namely, upon "Et exsultavit," etc.[18]

The composer is at liberty to write any one of the verses in the middle for fewer voices, and actually the usual thing is, in composing upon the odd-numbered verses, beginning with "Anima mea Dominum," to take the verse "Et misericordia eius" or "Deposuit potentes," but in composing upon the even-numbered verses, beginning with "Et exsultavit," to take as a rule the verse "Fecit potentiam" or "Esurientes implevit bonis." In the texture of these verses one uses greater industry and artifice, as was pointed out in section 10 of the chapter before last, in speaking of the sections of the mass that are usually written for fewer voices.

Thus all these particulars should be observed in composing the Magnificat, Benedictus, and Nunc dimittis.

Of the imitations and mediations and of the initial, medial, and final cadences of the psalms and canticles we shall treat in the book on the tones of figured music.

---

18 In their polyphonic settings of the gospel canticles, the composers of the sixteenth century usually restrict themselves to alternate verses, leaving the remainder of the text to be chanted in unison. Thus, when the odd-numbered verses are set, "Gloria Patri" will be choral, "Sicut erat" unison; when the even-numbered verses (beginning with Verse 2, "Et exsultavit") are set, "Gloria Patri" will be unison, "Sicut erat" choral.

16. ON THE MANNER OF COMPOSING HYMNS AND THE LAMENTA-
TIONS OF HOLY WEEK

Of the hymn there is nothing to be said except that it too is composed upon the plainsong with much solemnity, much artifice, and many repetitions (unless it is intended to be sung while walking in procession or on days of no solemnity); that the more it paraphrases the plainsong, the more beautiful it will be and the more carats it will have; and that any one of the verses in the middle may be sung with fewer voices, the last one for more voices (if so desired), in the manner spoken of in connection with the canticles.

The style for composing the Lamentations is such that all the parts proceed with gravity and modesty, nearly always singing together with such notes as the long, breve, semibreve, and minim, one part alone sometimes singing a few semiminims taken by step. In this kind of composition, more than in any other, the composer makes use of dissonances, suspensions, and harsh passages to make his work more doleful and mournful, as the sense of the words and the significance of the season demand. The usual custom is to compose them in the untransposed second, fourth, and sixth tones, these tones being naturally sad and doleful, and they are always sung by very low and heavy voices (only male voices taking part), with only one voice to a part. Of all varieties of composition, know that this is one of the most difficult to write judiciously and to make appropriate to the season and to the sense of the words. In each tone the positions of the initial, medial, and final cadences are the same as those of masses and motets (but with fewer divisions); those of the psalms and canticles are here of no use at all, for they usually end with the mediation of the verse or in accordance with the differences of the Seculorum.

In all the varieties of composition thus far explained, the syncopated minim and quaver are out of place, equally so the semiminim rest, for these, as I have pointed out at various times, are elements opposed to the gravity, majesty, and devout character required by ecclesiastical music, for all that many do the opposite today, either because they lack the knowledge necessary to the finished composer and excellent musician, or because, having it, they use it only to delight the sensual and to attract with their *firinfinfin* the vulgar throng.

8. Thomas Morley

One of the leading masters of the Elizabethan madrigal school and a remarkable musical theorist, Thomas Morley was born in 1557. He became a pupil of William Byrd, and in 1588 was awarded the degree of Mus.Bac. at Oxford. Subsequently, he became organist at St. Paul's in London and entered the Chapel Royal. He died in 1603.

Morley is particularly important as a composer of secular music; his madrigals, canzonets, ballets, and virginal pieces are remarkable for their consummate workmanship as well as for the grace and freshness of their melodic invention. Morley also left works of value in the field of religious music. His book, *A Plain and Easy Introduction to Practical Music* (1597), is one of the best-organized and most useful among sixteenth-century treatises.

From A Plain and Easy Introduction to Practical Music [1]

[*1597*]

THIS MUCH for motets, under which I comprehend all grave and sober music. The light music hath been of late more deeply dived into, so that there is no vanity which in it hath not been followed to the full, but the best kind of it is termed madrigal, a word for the etymology of which I can give no reason, yet use showeth that it is a kind of music made upon songs and sonnets such as Petrarcha and many other poets of our time have excelled in.

This kind of music were not so much disallowable if the poets who compose the ditties would abstain from some obscenities which all honest

---

1 Text: The original edition (London, 1597), as reproduced in *Shakespeare Association Facsimiles*, XIV (London, 1937), 179–181.

ears abhor, and sometimes from blasphemies to such as this, "ch'altro di te iddio non voglio," [2] which no man (at least who hath any hope of salvation) can sing without trembling. As for the music, it is next unto the motet the most artificial and to men of understanding most delightful. If therefore you will compose in this kind, you must possess yourself of an amorous humor (for in no composition shall you prove admirable except you put on and possess yourself wholly with that vein wherein you compose), so that you must in your music be wavering like the wind, sometimes wanton, sometimes drooping, sometimes grave and staid, otherwhile effeminate; you may maintain points [3] and revert them, [4] use triplas, [5] and show the very uttermost of your variety, and the more variety you show the better shall you please. In this kind our age excelleth, so that if you imitate any I would appoint you these for guides: Alfonso Ferrabosco for deep skill, Luca Marenzio for good air and fine invention, Horatio Vecchi, Stephàno Venturi, Ruggiero Giovanelli, and John Croce, with divers others who are very good, but not so generally good as these.

The second degree of gravity in this light music is given to canzonets, that is, little short songs, wherein little art can be showed, being made in strains, the beginning of which is some point lightly touched, and every strain repeated except the middle, which is in composition of the music a counterfeit of the madrigal.

Of the nature of these are the Neapolitans, or *canzoni a la Napoletana,* different from them in nothing save in name, so that whosoever knoweth the nature of the one must needs know the other also, and if you think them worthy of your pains to compose them, you have a pattern of them in Luca Marenzio and John Ferretti, who as it should seem hath employed most of all his study that way.

The last degree of gravity (if they have any at all) is given to the *villanelle,* or country songs, which are made only for the ditty's sake, for, so they be aptly set to express the nature of the ditty, the composer (though he were never so excellent) will not stick to take many perfect chords of one kind together, for in this kind they think it no fault (as being a kind of keeping decorum) to make a clownish music to a clownish

---

2 "Other than thee I'll have no god" (in an erotic context).

3 "We call that [a point or] a fugue when one part beginneth and the other singeth the same for some number of notes (which the first did sing)."—p. ˙6.

4 "The reverting of a point (which also we term a revert) is when a point is made rising or

falling and then turned to go the contrary way as many notes as it did at first."—p. 85.

5 "Is that which diminisheth the value of the notes to one third part: for three breves are set for one, and three semibreves for one, and is known when two numbers are set before the song, whereof the one containeth the other thrice, thus: ¾, ⁹⁄₆, ⁹⁄₃."—p. 29.

matter, and though many times the ditty be fine enough, yet because it carrieth that name *villanella* they take those disallowances as being good enough for plow and cart.

There is also another kind more light than this which they term *balletti*, or dances, and are songs which being sung to a ditty may likewise be danced; these and all other kinds of light music saving the madrigal are by a general name called airs. There be also another kind of ballets, commonly called fa las (the first set of that kind which I have seen was made by Gastoldi; if others have labored in the same field I know not), but a slight kind of music it is, and as I take it devised to be danced to voices.

The slightest kind of music (if they deserve the name of music) are the *vinate*, or drinking songs, for as I said before there is no kind of vanity whereunto they have not applied some music or other, as they have framed this to be sung in their drinking, but that vice being so rare among the Italians and Spaniards, I rather think that music to have been devised by or for the Germans (who in swarms do flock to the University of Italy) rather than for the Italians themselves.

There is likewise a kind of songs (which I had almost forgotten) called *Giustinianas* and are all written in the Bergamasca language. A wanton and rude kind of music it is and like enough to carry the name of some notable courtesan of the city of Bergamo, for no man will deny that Giustiniana is the name of a woman.[6]

There be also many other kinds of songs which the Italians make, as *pastorellas* and *passamezos* with a ditty and such like, which it would be both tedious and superfluous to delate unto you in words. Therefore I will leave to speak any more of them and begin to declare unto you those kinds which they make without ditties.

The most principal and chiefest kind of music which is made without a ditty is the fantasy, that is, when a musician taketh a point at his pleasure and wresteth and turneth it as he list, making either much or little of it as shall seem best in his own conceit. In this may more art be shown than in any other music, because the composer is tied to nothing but that he may add, diminish, and alter at his pleasure. And this kind will bear any allowances whatsoever tolerable in other music, except changing the air and leaving the key, which in fantasy may never be suffered. Other things you may use at your pleasure, as bindings with

6 Morley's naive definition is wholly misleading. Strictly speaking, the *giustiniana* is a specifically Venetian form of the *mascherata;* the three singers, who invariably stutter, introduce themselves as old men in love; see Alfred Einstein, "The Greghesca and the Giustiniana of the Sixteenth Century," *Journal of Renaissance and Baroque Music,* I (1946–47), 19–32.

discords, quick motions, slow motions, proportions, and what you list. Likewise this kind of music is with them who practise instruments of parts in greatest use, but for voices it is but seldom used.

The next in gravity and goodness unto this is called a pavan, a kind of staid music, ordained for grave dancing, and most commonly made of three strains, whereof every strain is played or sung twice. A strain they make to contain 8, 12, or 16 semibreves as they list, yet fewer than eight I have not seen in any pavan. In this you may not so much insist in following the point as in a fantasy, but it shall be enough to touch it once and so away to some close. Also in this you must cast your music by four, so that if you keep that rule it is no matter how many fours you put in your strain, for it will fall out well enough in the end, the art of dancing being come to that perfection that every reasonable dancer will make measure of no measure, so that it is no great matter of what number you make your strain.

After every pavan we usually set a galliard (that is, a kind of music made out of the other), causing it to go by a measure which the learned call *trochaicam rationem*, consisting of a long and a short stroke successively, for as the foot *trochaeus* consisteth of one syllable of two times and another of one time, so is the first of these two strokes double to the latter, the first being in time of a semibreve and the latter of a minim. This is a lighter and more stirring kind of dancing than the pavan, consisting of the same number of strains, and look how many fours of semibreves you put in the strain of your pavan, so many times six minims must you put in the strain of your galliard. The Italians make their galliards (which they term *saltarelli*) plain, and frame ditties to them which in their mascarados they sing and dance, and many times without any instruments at all, but instead of instruments they have courtesans disguised in men's apparel who sing and dance to their own songs.

The alman is a more heavy dance than this (fitly representing the nature of the people whose name it carrieth), so that no extraordinary motions are used in dancing of it. It is made of strains, sometimes two, sometimes three, and every strain is made by four, but you must mark that the four of the pavan measure is in dupla proportion to the four of the alman measure, so that as the usual pavan containeth in a strain the time of sixteen semibreves, so the usual alman contains the time of eight, and most commonly in short notes.

Like unto this is the French *branle* (which they call *branle simple*), which goeth somewhat rounder in time than this, otherwise the measure is all one. The *branle de Poitou*, or *branle double*, is more quick in time (as being in a round tripla), but the strain is longer, containing most usually twelve whole strokes.

Like unto this (but more light) be the *voltes* and *courantes*, which being both of a measure are notwithstanding danced after sundry fashions, the *volte* rising and leaping, the *courante* trevising and running, in which measure also our country dance is made, though it be danced after another form than any of the former. All these be made in strains, either two or three, as shall seem best to the maker, but the *courante* has twice so much in a strain as the English country dance.

There be also many other kinds of dances (as hornpipes, jigs, and infinite more) which I cannot nominate unto you, but knowing these the rest cannot but be understood, as being one with some of these which I have already told you.

II

Music in Renaissance Life
and Thought

9. Baldassare Castiglione

Born in 1478 near Mantua, the descendant of an old and distinguished family, Baldassare Castiglione is one of the representative figures of the Italian Renaissance. He served various princely courts and in 1525 went to Spain as an envoy of the Pope to the court of Charles V. He died at Toledo in 1529.

Castiglione is the author of poetry in Italian and Latin, and his letters are important as source material for the history of his time. His claim to lasting fame, however, rests upon *Il cortegiano* (1528), in which he endeavors to draw, in dialogues of great vivacity, a picture of the ideal courtier, giving at the same time a colorful description of contemporary society. The book professes to be an account of discussions held at the Ducal Palace in Urbino on four evenings in March 1507, each of the four books corresponding to one evening. The personages depicted are all more or less conspicuous historical figures, psychologically individualized and characterized. Castiglione leaves no doubt about the importance that music, song, and dance assumed at the court of Urbino and in the cultural frame of Renaissance society in general.

From Il cortegiano [1]

[*1528*]

[Translated by Sir Thomas Hoby, 1561]

AT THIS they all laughed. And the Count, beginning afresh:

"My lords (quoth he), you must think I am not pleased with the Courtier if he be not also a musician, and besides his understanding and cunning upon the book, have skill in like manner on sundry instruments. For if we weigh it well, there is no ease of the labors and medicines of

---

[1] Text: The reprint of the original edition of the translation of Sir Thomas Hoby (London, 1561), as published in *Tudor Translations,* XXIII (London, 1900). Castiglione's *Cortegiano* was written in 1514 and first published in 1528. I have made some use of the notes of Michele Scherillo (Milan, 1928).

feeble minds to be found more honest and more praiseworthy in time of leisure than it. And principally in courts, where (beside the refreshing of vexations that music bringeth unto each man) many things are taken in hand to please women withal, whose tender and soft breasts are soon pierced with melody and filled with sweetness. Therefore no marvel that in the old days and nowadays they have always been inclined to musicians, and counted this a most acceptable food of the mind."

Then the Lord Gaspar:

"I believe music (quoth he) together with many other vanities is meet for women, and peradventure for some also that have the likeness of men, but not for them that be men indeed; who ought not with such delicacies to womanish their minds and bring themselves in that sort to dread death."

"Speak it not," answered the Count. "For I shall enter into a large sea of the praise of music and call to rehearsal how much it hath always been renowned among them of old time and counted a holy matter; [2] and how it hath been the opinion of most wise philosophers that the world is made of music, and the heavens in their moving make a melody, and our soul framed after the very same sort, and therefore lifteth up itself and (as it were) reviveth the virtues and force of it with music. Wherefore it is written that Alexander was sometime so fervently stirred with it that (in a manner) against his will he was forced to arise from banquets and run to weapon, afterward the musician changing the stroke and his manner of tune, pacified himself again and returned from weapon to banqueting.[3] And I shall tell you that grave Socrates when he was well stricken in years learned to play upon the harp.[4] And I remember I have understood that Plato and Aristotle will have a man that is well brought up, to be also a musician; and declare with infinite reasons the force of music to be to very great purpose in us, and for many causes (that should be too long to rehearse) ought necessarily to be learned from a man's childhood, not only for the superficial melody that is heard, but to be sufficient to bring into us a new habit that is good and a custom inclining to virtue, which maketh the mind more apt to the conceiving of felicity, even as bodily exercise maketh the body more lusty, and not only hurteth not civil matters and warlike affairs, but is a

---

2 Quintilian, *Institutio oratoria*, I, x, 9.

3 Variously reported, although not in this form, by Seneca, Dio Chrysostom, Plutarch, and Suidas, the musician being sometimes Xenophantes, sometimes Timotheus, and sometimes Antigenedes. As told by Castiglione and other writers of his time the story appears to come ultimately from St. Basil, *Ad adolescentes* (PG, XXXI,

580): "When on one occasion Timotheus played on the aulos in Phrygian to Alexander, it is said that he roused him to arms during the banqueting and, when he had relaxed the harmony, brought him back to the guests again." For the version of Suidas, see note 23, p. 129 below.

4 Quintilian, *op. cit.*, I, x, 14.

great stay to them. Also Lycurgus in his sharp laws allowed music.[5] And it is read that the Lacedemons, which were valiant in arms, and the Cretenses used harps and other soft instruments; [6] and many most excellent captains of old time (as Epaminondas) gave themselves to music; and such as had not a sight in it (as Themistocles) were a great deal the less set by.[7] Have you not read that among the first instructions which the good old man Chiron taught Achilles in his tender age, whom he had brought up from his nurse and cradle, music was one? And the wise master would have those hands that should shed so much Trojan blood to be oftentimes occupied in playing upon the harp? What soldier is there (therefore) that will think it a shame to follow Achilles, omitting many other famous captains that I could allege? Do ye not then deprive our Courtier of music, which doth not only make sweet the minds of men, but also many times wild beasts tame; and whoso savoreth it not, a man may assuredly think him not to be well in his wits. Behold, I pray you, what force it hath, that in times past allured a fish to suffer a man to ride upon him through the tempestuous sea. We may see it used in the holy temples to render laud and thanks unto God, and it is a credible matter that it is acceptable unto Him, and that He hath given it unto us for a most sweet lightening of our travails and vexations. So that many times the boisterous laborers in the fields in the heat of the sun beguile their pain with rude and carterlike singing. With this the unmannerly countrywoman that ariseth before day out of her sleep to spin and card, defendeth herself and maketh her labor pleasant. This is the most sweet pastime after rain, wind, and tempest unto the miserable mariners. With this do the weary pilgrims comfort themselves in their troublesome and long voyages. And oftentimes prisoners in adversity, in fetters, and in stocks. In like manner for a greater proof that the tunableness of music (though it be but rude) is a very great refreshing of all worldly pains and griefs, a man would judge that nature had taught it unto nurses for a special remedy to the continual wailings of sucking babes, which at the sound of their voices fall into a quiet and sweet sleep, forgetting the tears that are so proper to them, and given us of nature in that age for a guess of the rest of our life to come." [8]

Here the Count pausing awhile the Lord Julian said:

"I am not of the Lord Gaspar's opinion, but I believe for the reasons you allege and for many others, that music is not only an ornament, but

5 Ibid., I, x, 15.
6 Often reported; cf. Plutarch, De musica, xxvi, and Athenaeus, 626B (S.R. I, 50 and 52).

7 Cicero, Tusculan Disputations, I, ii, 4.
8 St. John Chrysostom, Exposition of Psalm XLI (S.R. I, 67–69).

also necessary for a Courtier. But I would have you declare how this and the other qualities which you appoint him are to be practised, and at what time, and in what sort. Because many things that of themselves be worthy praise, oftentimes in practising them out of season seem most foolish. And contrariwise, some things that appear to be of small moment, in the well applying them are greatly esteemed."

. . . . .

"Methink," answered Sir Frederick, "pricksong is a fair music, so it be done upon the book surely and after a good sort. But to sing to the lute [9] is much better, because all the sweetness consisteth in one alone, and a man is much more heedful and understandeth better the feat manner and the air or vein of it when the ears are not busied in hearing any more than one voice; and beside, every little error is soon perceived, which happeneth not in singing with company, for one beareth out another. But singing to the lute with the ditty [10] (methink) is more pleasant than the rest, for it addeth to the words such a grace and strength that it is a great wonder. Also all instruments with frets [11] are full of harmony, because the tunes of them are very perfect, and with ease a man may do many things upon them that fill the mind with the sweetness of music. And the music of a set of viols [12] doth no less delight a man, for it is very sweet and artificial. A man's breast giveth a great ornament and grace to all these instruments, in the which I will have it sufficient that our Courtier have an understanding. Yet the more cunning he is upon them, the better it is for him, without meddling much with the instruments that Minerva and Alcibiades refused,[13] because it seemeth they are noisome. Now as touching the time and season when these sorts of music are to be practised, I believe at all times when a man is in familiar and loving company, having nothing else ado. But especially they are meet to be practised in the presence of women, because those sights sweeten the minds of the hearers and make them the more apt to be pierced with the pleasantness of music, and also they quicken the spirits of the very doers. I am well pleased (as I have said) they flee the multitude, and especially of the unnoble. But the seasoning of the whole must be discretion, because in effect it were a matter unpossible to imagine all cases that fall. And if the Courtier be a righteous judge of himself, he

---

9 Castiglione has *il cantare alla viola.*
10 Castiglione has *il cantare alla viola per recitare.*
11 Castiglione has 'all keyboard instruments" (*tutti gli instrumenti di tasti*).

12 Castiglione has *quattro viole da arco.*
13 The auloi; for the story, see Plutarch, *Life of Alcibiades.*

shall apply himself well enough to the time and shall discern when the hearers' minds are disposed to give ear and when they are not. He shall know his age, for (to say the truth) it were no meet matter, but an ill sight to see a man of any estimation being old, hoarheaded and tooth-less, full of wrinkles, with a lute in his arms [14] playing upon it and sing-ing in the midst of a company of women, although he could do it reason-ably well. And that because such songs contain in them words of love, and in old men love is a thing to be jested at, although otherwhile he seemeth among other miracles of his to take delight in spite of years to set afire frozen hearts."

Then answered the Lord Julian:

"Do you not bar poor old men from this pleasure, Sir Frederick, for in my time I have known men of years have very perfect breasts and most nimble fingers for instruments, much more than some young men."

"I go not about," quoth Sir Frederick, "to bar old men from this pleasure, but I will bar you these ladies from laughing at that folly. And in case old men will sing to the lute,[15] let them do it secretly, and only to rid their minds of those troublesome cares and grievous disquietings that our life is full of and to taste of that excellence which I believe Pythagoras and Socrates favored in music. And set case they exercise it not at all, for that they have gotten a certain habit and custom of it, they shall savor it much better in hearing than he that hath no knowl-edge in it. For like as the arms of a smith that is weak in other things, because they are more exercised, be stronger than another body's that is sturdy but not exercised to work with his arms, even so the ears that be exercised in music do much better and sooner discern it and with much more pleasure judge of it than other, how good and quick soever they be, that have not been practised in the variety of pleasant music; because those musical tunes pierce not, but without leaving any taste of themselves, pass by the ears not accustomed to hear them, although the very wild beasts feel some delight in melody. This is therefore the pleasure meet for old men to take in music. The selfsame I say of danc-ing, for indeed these exercises ought to be left of before age constraineth us to leave them whether we will or no."

. . . . .

---

[14] Castiglione has *con una viola in braccio.*   [15] Castiglione has *cantare alla viola.*

10. Pierre de Ronsard

The great French poet was born in 1524 and died in 1585. Ronsard strove to bring about a rebirth of lyric poetry in the ancient Greek sense of the term, as a musical expression of the soul in a state of emotion. As this ideal could be achieved only by a close co-operation of music and poetry, Ronsard set all his efforts in this direction. Thus, to the collected poems which appeared under the title *Les amours* (1552) he added a musical supplement containing settings of his poems by various musicians of the time. Considering Ronsard's views on the union of music and poetry, it is not surprising that he was one of the poets whose works were most frequently set to music. There exist entire collections of Ronsard's poems set to music by Philippe de Monte, Antoine de Bertrand, and other contemporary composers; but his verses are also found in a great number of miscellaneous collections of polyphonic chansons of the sixteenth century with musical settings by Jannequin, Goudimel, Certon, Lassus, Le Jeune, Costeley, etc. Important as a sort of manifesto is Ronsard's dedication to François II, prefixed to the *Livre des mélanges*, published in 1560 by Le Roy and Ballard.

Livre des mélanges [1]

[*1560*]

DEDICATION

EVEN, SIRE, as by the touchstone one tries gold, whether it be good or bad, so the ancients tried by music the spirits of those who are noble and magnanimous, not straying from their first essence, and of those who are numbed, slothful, and bastardized in this mortal body, no more

---

1 Text: *Oeuvres complètes,* ed. by Paul Laumonier (Paris, 1914-19), VII, 16-20. Laumonier gives the text of 1572; I have preferred to translate the text of 1560, which is easily restored with the help of Laumonier's note (see note 5, p. 99 below).

remembering the celestial harmony of heaven than the comrades of Ulysses, after Circe had turned them into swine, remembered that they had been men. For he, Sire, that hearing a sweet accord of instruments or the sweetness of the natural voice feels no joy and no agitation and is not thrilled from head to foot, as being delightfully rapt and somehow carried out of himself—'tis the sign of one whose soul is tortuous, vicious, and depraved, and of whom one should beware, as not fortunately born. For how could one be in accord with a man who by nature hates accord? He is unworthy to behold the sweet light of the sun who does not honor music as being a small part of that which, as Plato says, so harmoniously animates the whole great universe. Contrariwise, he who does honor and reverence to music is commonly a man of worth, sound of soul, by nature loving things lofty, philosophy, the conduct of affairs of state, the tasks of war, and in brief, in all honorable offices he ever shows the sparks of his virtue.

Now to tell here what music is; whether it is governed more by inspiration than by art; to tell of its concords, its tones, modulations, voices, intervals, sounds, systems, and transformations; of its division into enharmonic, which for its difficulty was never perfectly in use; into chromatic, which for its lasciviousness was by the ancients banished from republics; into diatonic, which was by all approved, as approaching nearest to the melody of the macrocosm; to speak of the Phrygian, Dorian, and Lydian music; and how certain peoples of Greece went bravely into battle inspired by harmony, as do our soldiers today to the sounds of drums and trumpets; how King Alexander was roused to fury by the songs of Timotheus, and how Agamemnon, going to Troy, left on purpose in his house I know not what Dorian musician, who by the virtue of the anapestic foot tempered the unbridled amorous passions of his wife Clytaemnestra, inflamed with love of whom Aegisthus could never attain to enjoyment until he had wickedly put the musician to death; to wish further to deduce how all things, as well in the heavens and in the sea as on the earth, are composed of accords, measures, and proportions; to wish to discuss how the most honorable persons of past ages, monarchs, princes, philosophers, governors of provinces, and captains of renown, were curiously enamored of the ardors of music; I should never have done; the more so as music has always been the sign and the mark of those who have shown themselves virtuous, magnanimous, and truly born to feel nothing vulgar.

For example I shall take solely the late King your father,[2] may God

---

[2] Henri II.

absolve him, who during his reign made it apparent how liberally Heaven had endowed him with all graces and with gifts rare among kings; who surpassed, not only in grandeur of empire, but in clemency, liberality, goodness, piety, and religion, not only all the princes his predecessors, but all who have ever lived that have borne that honorable title of king; who, in order to reveal the stars of his high birth and to show that he was perfect in all virtues, so honored, loved, and esteemed music that all in France who today remain well-disposed toward this art, have not, all combined, so much affection for it as he had alone.

You also, Sire, as the inheritor both of his realm and of his virtues, show that you are his son, favored by Heaven, in so perfectly loving this science and its accords, without which nothing of this world could remain whole.

Now to tell you here of Orpheus, of Terpander, of Eumolpus, of Arion, these are stories with which I do not wish to burden the paper, as things well known to you. I will relate to you only that anciently the kings most eminent for virtue caused their children to be brought up in the houses of musicians, as did Peleus, who sent his son Achilles, and Aeson, who sent his son Jason, to the venerated cave of the centaur Chiron to be instructed as well in arms as in medicine and in the art of music, the more so as these three professions, joined together, are not unbefitting the grandeur of a prince; and there were given by Achilles and Jason, who were princes of your age,[3] such commendable examples of virtue that the one was honored by the divine poet Homer as sole author of the taking of Troy, and the other was celebrated by Apollonius of Rhodes as the first who taught the sea to endure the unknown burden of ships; and after he had passed the rocks Symplegades and tamed the fury of the cold Scythian Sea, he returned to his country enriched by the noble fleece of gold. Therefore, Sire, these two princes will be to you as patrons of virtue, and when sometimes you are wearied by your most urgent affairs, you will imitate them by lightening your cares with the accords of music, in order to return the fresher and the better-disposed to the royal burden which you support with such adroitness.

Your Majesty should not marvel if this book of miscellanies, which is very humbly dedicated to you by your very humble and obedient servants and printers Adrian Le Roy and Robert Ballard, is composed of the oldest songs that can today be found,[4] because the music of the ancients has

---

3 François II, husband of Mary Queen of Scots, was sixteen years old on January 19, 1560, and died on December 5 of the same year.
4 The composers most frequently represented are Willaert, Gombert, Lassus, Josquin, Leschenet, Arcadelt, Crequillon, Mouton, Certon, and Maillard.

always been esteemed the most divine, the more so since it was composed in a happier age, less contaminated by the vices which reign in this last age of iron. Moreover, the divine inspirations of music, poetry, and painting do not arrive at perfection by degrees, like the other sciences, but by starts, and like flashes of lightning, one here, another there, appear in various lands, then suddenly vanish. And for that reason, Sire, when some excellent worker in this art reveals himself, you should guard him with care, as being something so excellent that it rarely appears. Of such men have arisen within six or seven score years Josquin Desprez, a native of Hainaut, and his disciples Mouton, Willaert, Richafort, Jannequin, Maillard, Claudin, Moulu, Certon,[5] and Arcadelt, who in the perfection of this art does not yield to the ancients, from being inspired by Charles, Cardinal of Lorraine, his Apollo.

Many other things might be said of music, which Plutarch and Boethius have amply mentioned. But neither the brevity of this preface, nor the convenience of time, nor the subject permits me to discourse of it at greater length. Entreating the Creator, Sire, to increase more and more the virtues of Your Majesty and to continue you in the kindly affection which you are pleased to have for music and for all those who study to make flourish again under your sway the sciences and arts which flourished under the empire of Caesar Augustus, of which Augustus may it be God's will to grant you the years, the virtues, and the prosperity.

---

[5] For the remainder of this paragraph the edition of 1572 substitutes the following: ". . . and Arcadelt, and now the more than divine Orlando, who like a bee has sipped all the most beautiful flowers of the ancients and moreover seems alone to have stolen the harmony of the heavens to delight us with it on earth, surpassing the ancients and making himself the unique wonder of our time."

11. Giovanni de' Bardi

Born in Florence in 1534, descended from a wealthy family, a devoted amateur of the arts and an earnest student of music and poetry, Giovanni de' Bardi was in a position to dedicate himself almost exclusively to the work in which he was primarily interested, i.e., to bring about a musical renascence that would correspond to the humanistic spirit of the Renaissance. To attain this goal, Bardi gathered at his home in Florence the most prominent scholars and artists of the city—the so-called "Camerata"—and collaborated in the first experiments in conscious imitation of ancient Greek tragedy, experiments that were to result in the birth of a new art-form, the opera. Of the numerous documents bearing on the first experiments, the present discourse is perhaps the very earliest. It purports to be the work of Bardi himself; in reality, it will perhaps have been written for him by Galilei or some other member of his circle.

In 1592 Bardi abandoned Florence for Rome where he became chamberlain at the papal court, leaving his work in Florence to be continued by others.

Discourse on Ancient Music and Good Singing

ADDRESSED TO GIULIO CACCINI, CALLED ROMANO [1]

[ca. 1580]

SINCE I think that I shall be doing a thing not unpleasing to you, my very dear Signor Giulio Caccini, if I collect one by one the countless discussions of music which we have had together in various places and at various times and bind them up, like a little sheaf gleaned from the field of your intellect, I shall do it in such a way that you may comprehend

1 Text: As published in G. B. Doni, *Lyra Barberina* (Florence, 1763), II, 233-248. I have omitted two passages of secondary interest.

and consider them in one view, like a united and well-proportioned body. And I take pleasure in holding the present brief discourse, like those former ones, with you, for having been associated from your youth with so many noble and gifted members of the Florentine Academy, you have (not only in my opinion, but also in the opinion of those who understand the true and perfect music) reached such a point that there is not a man in Italy who surpasses you, nay, few—perhaps not one—who equals you.

I speak of that sort of music which today is sung to instruments, either in company with others, or alone. It would take too long and would perhaps become tedious to you and to him who reads this my discourse, were I to treat one by one of its principles and of the great men who have taken part in it, of whom to my knowledge at least fifty became great philosophers or most polished reciters of poetry. Thus I shall not stop now to tell of the wealth of instruments that these great scholars had. But, in order that I may well express their ideas, I shall treat very briefly of who it was that defined this music, of the twenty-seven tunings [2] that the ancients had, and of the seven modes that they called "harmonies," [3] like the architect who, to finish the house that he has planned in his mind, first provides himself with everything he needs for his labor. Thus the beginning of my discourse will be the definition of this music. For just as one could have only a poor notion of what a man is if one did not know that a man is an animal rational, visible, and sociable, or of what a city is if one did not know that a city is a union of a number of houses and quarters situated in one place in order that men may live well and justly, so one cannot pass judgment on practical music and on good singing if one does not know what sort of thing this music is.

---

[2] " 'Tuning' (*spartimento* or *distribuzione*) means to indicate by an exact number the difference between the semitone and the tone, and thus between one tone and another, in vocal and instrumental music" (p. 235 of the original).

[3] "To each of the seven species of the octave the ancients assigned a tone (by them called a 'harmony'), and these tones differed from one another not only in species but also in being sung each at its own pitch—low, intermediate, or high; thus some were sung and played in the lower notes of the double octave, others in the intermediate, and others in the higher, as will be seen in the demonstration we shall give of the seven tones" (p. 237 of the original). In this demonstration (p. 239 of the original), which is concerned solely with the teachings of Ptolemy, Bardi writes out the seven species of the double octave as a descending series (Hypodorian as highest, Mixolydian as lowest) and goes on to explain that, as actually sung, these form an ascending series with the Hypodorian as the lowest; a tone above this is the Hypophrygian, a tone above this the Hypolydian, and a semitone above this the Dorian, which is sung in the *quintadecima ordinaria* (A to a'); Phrygian, Lydian, and Mixolydian follow at the intervals tone, tone, and semitone. Up to a certain point Bardi presents the Ptolemaic teaching correctly: the species are correctly named and identified and the pitch-relationships of the *mesai* correctly stated. But the final outcome is an elaborate misunderstanding: *mese* is for Bardi always the Ptolemaic or "thetic" *mese;* thus his keys ascend, not by tone and semitone, but by thirds. Expressed in terms of our key-signatures, Bardi's identifications amount to this: Hypodorian, 2 sharps; Hypophrygian, 6 sharps; Hypolydian, 3 sharps; Dorian, no signature; Phrygian, 4 sharps; Lydian, 8 sharps; Mixolydian, 2 flats. It may be added that Galilei offers a similar but not identical misinterpretation of the Ptolemaic teaching in his *Dialogo della musica antica e della moderna* (Venice, 1581).

Music is defined by Plato in the third book of his *Republic*,[4] where he says that it is a combination of words and harmony and rhythm. But in order that the terms "harmony" and "rhythm" may be thoroughly understood, we shall briefly define them as well as we can.

Harmony is a general term, and in speaking of it, Pythagoras says, and after him Plato, that the world is composed of it. But let us come to the particular and treat of the harmony of music as defined by Plato, which harmony, according to Pausanias,[5] takes its name from Harmonia, the wife of Cadmus, at whose wedding the Muses sang. Harmony then is the proportion of the low and the high, and of words in rhythm, that is, well arranged with respect to the long and the short. And harmony is likewise in musical instruments, for in these too are the low, the high, and the intermediate, and also rhythm, that is, faster or slower movement of the long and the short.[6] Again, harmony may be composed of all these things combined, that is, of words well sung and having, as their accompaniment, this or that instrument.

Rhythm is likewise a general term, and in defining it, Aristides Quintilianus says that it is a system of times arranged in certain orders, a system being simply an ordering of things.[7] Discussing rhythm, Plato says that it is divided into three species, progressing either by harmony, or by bodily movement, or by words, bodily rhythm being manifest to the eye, the other two species to the ear.[8] But let us come to the rhythm of music, which is simply giving time to words that are sung as long and short, and as fast and slow, likewise to musical instruments.

Taken all together, these considerations show that practical music is a combination of words arranged by a poet into verses made up of various metres with respect to the long and the short, these being in their movement now fast and now slow, now low, now high, and now intermediate, approaching the sound of the words of the human voice, now sung by that voice alone, now accompanied by a musical instrument, which in turn should accompany the words with the long and the short, with fast and slow movement, and with the low, the high, and the intermediate.

Now that we have given the definition of music according to Plato (a definition in which Aristotle and the other scholars concur) and have said what music is, . . . let us turn to the marvels of music, in discussing which Damon, the teacher of Socrates, says that, being chaste, it has the

4 398D (*S.R.* I, 4).
5 *Description of Greece*, IX, xii, 3.
6 Plato, *Laws*, 665A, also *Symposium*, 187A-B, and *Philebus*, 17C.
7 Aristides Quintilianus, *De musica* (Meibom's ed., p. 31).
8 *Laws*, 672E-673A.

power of disposing our minds to virtue and, being the contrary, to vice.[9] And Plato says that there are two disciplines—one for the body, which is gymnastics, and one for the good of the mind, which is music; he also tells us that Thales the Milesian sang so sweetly that he not only influenced the minds of certain persons, but also cured illness and the plague.[10] And we read that Pythagoras cured drunkards with music, and Empedocles insane persons, and Socrates a man possessed.[11] And Plutarch tells us that Asclepiades cured delirious persons with the symphony, which is simply a mixture of song and sound.[12] And it is said that Ismenias cured sciatic persons and the fever with music.[11] And Aulus Gellius writes that those who suffered from sciatic gout were healed with the sound of the tibia, likewise those who had been bitten by serpents.[13]

But I should go far afield and beyond my intention if I were to give to music and all its marvels the praise that is their due, for my sole intention is to show you, as clearly as I can, how it is to be treated in practice. Thus, now that I have stated the definition of music and have said what rhythm is, and likewise harmony, both in general and in particular,[14] it is fitting that I show you how many and of what sort are the divisions of music and what their virtues are, for without discussing these things it would be difficult for me to attain the end that I have set before me.

I say, therefore, that the music of our times has two divisions—one which is called counterpoint and another which we shall call the art of good singing. The first of these is simply a combination of several melodies and of several modes sung at the same time—a combination, that is, of the low, the high, and the intermediate, and of the various rhythms of the several melodies. To take an example, if a madrigal is composed in four parts, then the bass will sing one melody, the tenor another, and the alto and soprano still other ones, different from theirs and in different modes. This we have shown above—we have shown, that is, that in every one of our musical compositions there are, in the low, the intermediate, and the high, various octave-species,[15] and various rhythms. And this, to take another example, because Messer Bass, soberly dressed in semibreves and minims, stalks through the ground-floor rooms of his

9 Aristides Quintilianus, *op. cit.*, (Meibom's ed., pp. 94–96).

10 *Laws*, 673A. Plato does not mention Thales the Milesian in a musical connection; Bardi is thinking, perhaps, of Plutarch's references to Thaletas (or Thales) of Crete.

11 Boethius, *De institutione musica*, I, i (*S.R.* I, 82–83).

12 Not said by Plutarch, but often reported by others; cf., for example, Censorinus, *In die natali*, xii, Martianus Capella, *Satyricon*, ix, Isidore of Seville, *Etymologiae*, IV. xiii.

13 *Attic Nights*, IV, xiii.

14 For Bardi's definition of harmony "in particular," see note 3, p. 101 above.

15 Page 237 of the original: "Another error in the music of our time is that two species of the octave are always sung in every composition; in the Second Tone, for example, the bass sings the octave beginning d *sol re* and the soprano its octave duplication."

palace while Soprano, decked out in minims and semiminims, walks hurriedly about the terrace at a rapid pace and Messers Tenor and Alto, with various ornaments and in habits different from the others, stray through the rooms of the intervening floors. For in truth it would seem a sin to the contrapuntists of today (may they be pardoned these mixtures of several melodies and several modes!)—it would seem, I say, a mortal sin if all the parts were heard to beat at the same time with the same notes, with the same syllables of the verse, and with the same longs and shorts; the more they make the parts move, the more artful they think they are. This, in my opinion, is the concern of the stringed instruments, for, there being no voice in these, it is fitting that the player, in playing airs not suited to singing or dancing—it is fitting, I say, that the player should make the parts move and that he should contrive canons, double counterpoints, and other novelties to avoid wearying his hearers. And I judge this to be the species of music so much condemned by the philosophers, especially by Aristotle in the Eighth Book of his *Politics*,[16] where he calls it artificial and wholly useless, except as a contrast to its rivals, and unworthy of a free man for lacking the power to move a man's mind to this or that moral quality. Elsewhere, speaking of this same subject, he says that a man cannot be called a good musician who lacks the power to dispose the mind of another with his harmony to any moral quality.

But since we are so much in the dark, let us at least endeavor to give poor unfortunate Music a little light, for from her decline until now, and this means ever so many centuries, she has had not one artificer who has at all considered her case, but has been treated in another way, inimical to her, that of counterpoint. This light may be permitted to reach her only little by little, just as a man who has been afflicted with a very serious illness ought properly to be restored step by step to his former state of health, taking little food, and that nourishing and easily digestible.

For the present, the little food that we shall give to Music shall be to endeavor not to spoil the verse, not imitating the musicians of today, who think nothing of spoiling it to pursue their ideas or of cutting it to bits to make nonsense of the words, like a man who does not mind that the robe made from the cloth that he has is short and ill-fitting or even that his large and conspicuous slippers happen to have been cut from it. For, to take an example, while the soprano sings "Voi che ascoltate in rime," [17] the bass at the same time sings other words, thus mixing one idea with

---

16 1341B (S.R. I, 22–23).   17 Petrarch, *Rime*, i, i.

another, which rightly considered is the torture and death of forsaken Music. This subject is discussed by all the great scholars and in particular by Plato, who says that the melody ought always to follow the verse that the poet has composed,[18] just as a good cook adds a little sauce or condiment to a dish that he has well seasoned, to make it seem more pleasing to his master.

In composing, then, you will make it your chief aim to arrange the verse well and to declaim the words as intelligibly as you can, not letting yourself be led astray by the counterpoint like a bad swimmer who lets himself be carried out of his course by the current and comes to shore beyond the mark that he had set, for you will consider it self-evident that, just as the soul is nobler than the body, so the words are nobler than the counterpoint. Would it not seem ridiculous if, walking in the public square, you saw a servant followed by his master and commanding him, or a boy who wanted to instruct his father or his tutor? The divine Cipriano, toward the end of his life, was well aware how very grave an error this was in the counterpoint of his day. For this reason, straining every fibre of his genius, he devoted himself to making the verse and the sound of the words thoroughly intelligible in his madrigals, as may be seen in one of those for five voices, "Poichè m'invita amore," [19] and in an earlier one, "Se bene il duolo," [20] and in still another, "Di virtù, di costume, di valore"; [21] also in those published very shortly before his death, in the one with the words "Un altra volta la Germania stride," in another beginning "O sonno, o della quiete umid'ombrosa," in "Schietto arbuscello," [22] and in the rest, by no means composed at haphazard. For this great man told me himself, in Venice, that this was the true manner of composing and a different one, and if he had not been taken from us by death, he would in my opinion have restored the music combining several melodies to a degree of perfection from which others might easily have returned it little by little to that true and perfect music so highly praised by the ancients.

But perhaps we have made too long a digression. So we shall say that, besides not spoiling the words, you will likewise not spoil the verse. Thus, wishing to set to music a madrigal or canzone or any other poem, you will carefully commit it to memory and consider whether the content

---

18 *Republic,* 400D (*S.R.* I, 7).

19 *Le Vive fiamme de'vaghi e dilettevoli madrigali* (Venice, 1565), No. 16.

20 Published in his *Quarto libro de' Madrigali a cinque voci* (Venice, 1557), No. 3 (quoted by Einstein in *The Italian Madrigal,* I, 420).

21 Published in his *Terzo libro de' Madrigali a cinque voci* (Venice, 1557).

22 *Il secondo libro de' Madrigali a quattro voci* (Venice, 1557), Nos. 1, 5, and 3. See the reprint by Gertrude Parker Smith, *Smith College Archives,* VI (Northampton, 1943).

is, for example, magnificent or plaintive. If it is magnificent, you will take the Dorian mode,[23] which begins on E *la mi* and has a *la mi re* as its mese, giving the entire melody to the tenor and turning about the mese as much as you can,[24] for (as we have said elsewhere) things that are sublime and magnificent are uttered in an agreeable and intermediate tone of voice. But if the content is plaintive, you will take the Mixolydian mode,[25] which begins on b *mi* and has e *la mi* as its mese; about this you will turn as much as you can, giving the principal melody to the soprano part. And in this way you will continue to regulate matters according to the other contents expressed in the words, always bearing in mind the nature of the slow, the fast, and the intermediate. Having, for example, to set to music the canzone beginning "Italia mia, ben che'l parlar sia indarno," [26] you will take the Dorian mode mentioned above, giving the principal melody to the tenor, turning about the mese, and so adapting the rhythm, that is, the long and the short, that it will be neither too slow nor too fast but will imitate the speech of a man magnificent and serious. And in considering other cases, you will proceed just as we have directed in this one.

But since it is the usual thing nowadays to enliven musical performances by adding to the voice the delicate melody of instruments, it will not be inappropriate if with all possible brevity I say something about these. I say, then, that musical instruments are of two sorts, being either wind instruments or stringed instruments; of those like the drum I find no science, for in them there is no musical sound, only a percussion.

Wind instruments, as more nearly imitating the human voice, are given preference over the others by Aristotle in his *Problems*.[27] But to discuss this point is not to our purpose. We shall simply say that among the wind instruments there are some for playing compositions that are low-pitched and somnolent—these are the trombones; others apt for playing those that are high-pitched and lively, such as the *cornetti;* still others apt for playing those usual ones that lie in the intermediate register, such as the flutes and *pifferi allemani*. But seeing that I have not sufficient grasp of the wind instruments to use suitably

23 By "the Dorian mode" Bardi means the octave species as from E to e, sung in the register E to e (see note 3, p. 101 above).
24 Bardi understands the Ptolemaic or "thetic" *mese* (the fourth step within each modal octave) to have had the function of a tonic or tonal center in the music of the Greeks.
25 By "the Mixolydian mode" Bardi means the octave species as from B to b, sung in the regis-

ter a to a' (2 flats); the mese is d (transposed e *la mi*). It is because of this relatively high register that Bardi now assigns the principal melody to the soprano, having previously directed that in Dorian compositions it should be given to the tenor.
26 Petrarch, *Rime*, cxxviii, 1.
27 XIX, xliii (922A).

those that I know, I defer to the judgment of those who are skilled in this profession.

Next come the stringed instruments, their strings worked in two sorts, although we use them in many forms. For part of them are of brass or of some other metal; the others, taken from animals, we call gut. Strings of gut are used for the viols and harps, also for the lute and such other instruments as are similar to it, and as more nearly resembling the human voice, they will be the better suited to the intermediate modes, like the Dorian; the same may be said of the viols, which have much of the grave and the magnificent. Strings of metal are used for the *gravicembali* and citherns, and as more effective in the higher harmonies than the above, can be played in the low, the high, and the intermediate.

Besides this, it is necessary to take great care in combining these instruments, for not all of them are tuned according to the same tuning, the viol and lute being tuned according to the tuning of Aristoxenus,[28] the harp and *gravicembalo* making their modulations with other intervals. And more than once I have felt like laughing when I saw musicians struggling to put a lute or viol into proper tune with a keyboard instrument, for aside from the octave these instruments have few strings in common that are in unison, a circumstance that may detract from their usefulness, since until now this highly important matter has gone unnoticed or, if noticed, unremedied. In your consorts, then, you will as far as possible avoid combining lutes or viols with keyboard instruments or harps or other instruments not tuned in unison, but in various ways.

Before concluding my discussion of instruments, I have thought to make known to you an idea that has often occurred to me. Since you are to be the source of an unparalleled music, I would have you skilled in playing upon an instrument some beautiful melody partaking of the sublime and magnificent, perhaps one such as that composed by the philosopher Memphis,[29] to the sound of which Socrates illustrated all

---

28 By "the tuning of Aristoxenus" Bardi means equal temperament, by "other intervals" the intervals of meantone temperament or intervals closely approximating these. Cf. Galilei, *Discorso intorno all'opere di messer Gioseffe Zarlino* (Florence, 1589), p. 116: "If there were no other impediment, it might well be that we should be satisfied with the fifth that we hear on the keyboard instruments, which is not only smaller than the sesquialtera fifth, but smaller than the fifth sounded by the lute, which is the same as that of Aristoxenus, differences which if slight are nonetheless perceptible. Thus it appears that in a sense the Pythagorean fifth is somewhat high and that of the keyboard instruments somewhat low, while that of the lute, lying between

these two, is the true one which, as we have said, is the same as that of Aristoxenus." Measured in "cents," the justly intoned (Pythagorean) fifth is 702, the equally tempered (Aristoxenian) fifth 700, the fifth of the meantone temperament 696.6.

29 Athenaeus, 20D: "The entire population of the world . . . united in naming the philosopher-dancer of our time (Agrippa, slave of Verus) 'Memphis,' quaintly comparing his bodily motions with the oldest and most royal of cities. . . . This 'Memphis' explains the nature of the Pythagorean system, expounding in silent mimicry all its doctrines to us more clearly than they who profess to teach eloquence." [Gulick]

the precepts of the Pythagorean philosophy without speaking a word. I add that, just as among Moors and Spanish women one may see shameless and wanton customs represented in music and dancing, so the virtuous and perfect musician can represent the contrary, that is, songs and dances filled with majesty and continence, as we read of that never-sufficiently-to-be-praised musician [30] who for so many years maintained the resolution of Penelope and preserved her from the importunity of her suitors until the wise and cunning Ulysses returned from his long exile to his native land.

But let us leave the sort of practical music that consists in good composing and playing and come to the sort that is used in good singing. This has two divisions—singing in company and singing alone. Thus, to bring our discussion to an end, we must again place before our eyes all that we have discussed thus far, for this is the foundation upon which our palace is to stand firm. Let us recall, then, that the tunings were devised by the ancient philosophers with the greatest care and in a determined number, since each sound in singing must fit its place exactly; that the same may be said of the highness and the lowness of the modes and of their quality, and of the distinctions of the octaves with their various semitones, and of the force of the harmonies that are low, intermediate, and high; that the Dorian mode, lying in the center of the sounds suited to human speech, was prized and revered more highly than the rest, while the lower and higher harmonies were less prized, the one being too sluggish, the other too agitated. We have shown that the verse is made up of the long and the short and that, in the opinion of Plato and others, the sound and the counterpoint (as we choose to call it) should follow the speech and not the contrary, and we have defined music, harmony, and rhythm.

· · · · · ·

Let us now speak of the great distinction that should be made between singing alone and singing in company and of how one should not imitate those who, when they sing in parts, as though the whole company had come only to hear their creaking, think only of making their own voices heard, not knowing or perhaps not remembering that good part-singing is simply joining one's voice with the voices of others and forming one body with these; the same may be said of those others who, to complete their passages, disregard the time, so breaking and stretching it that they

---

[30] Phemius.

make it altogether impossible for their colleagues to sing properly. The singer ought also to take care to enter softly after a rest, not imitating those who enter so noisily that they seem to be finding fault with you for some mistake, or those others who, to avoid the bass parts, sing so loudly in the high register that they seem like criers auctioning off the pledges of the unfortunate, like little snarling dogs stealing silently through the streets of others and imagining that they are making no end of noise.

When singing alone, whether to the lute or *gravicembalo* or to some other instrument, the singer may contract or expand the time at will, seeing that it is his privilege to regulate the time as he thinks fit. To make divisions upon the bass is not natural, for (as we have said) this part is by nature slow, low, and somnolent. Yet it is the custom to do this. I know not what to say of it and am not eager to praise or to blame it, but I would counsel you to do it as little as possible and, when you do, at least to make it clear that you do it to please someone, also taking care never to pass from the tenor to the bass, seeing that with its passages the bass takes away whatever magnificence and gravity the tenor, with its majesty, has bestowed.

Besides this, it is necessary to sing accurately and well, to give each tone and semitone its proper place, and to connect the sounds exactly. Rejecting the improper practices employed today by those who search for unusual sounds, you will seek to use only a few, turning about the mese of the mode and employing it as often as you can, bearing in mind that, in speaking, man seeks to use few sounds and seldom, perhaps never uses wide leaps unless stirred up by anger or some other violent passion. In this you will imitate the great musician Olympus, who, in the many hundreds of songs that he gave to the world, never touched more than four strings in the principal part.

Then you will bear in mind that the noblest function a singer can perform is that of giving proper and exact expression to the canzone as set down by the composer, not imitating those who aim only at being thought clever (a ridiculous pretension) and who so spoil a madrigal with their ill-ordered passages that even the composer himself would not recognize it as his creation.

Finally, the nice singer will endeavor to deliver his song with all the suavity and sweetness in his power, rejecting the notion that music must be sung boldly, for a man of this mind seems among other singers like a plum among oranges or like a man of fierce appearance showing the *giaro* among city dwellers and well-bred people. Speaking on this topic, Aristotle says in his *Politics* [31] that youths should be taught music as a thing seasoned with great sweetness; and Plato, that Thales the Milesian cured illness with his sweet manner of singing; and Macrobius, that, on leaving the body, the soul returns to its origin, which is heaven, through the sweetness of music; [32] and the poet:

> Musica dulcisono coelestia numina cantu [33]

with the rest of the passage; and Petrarch:

> Sweet song, O ladies virtuous and fair [34]

and at another time:

> Here sweetly sang and here sat down; [35]

and the divine poet Dante, in the second canto of his *Purgatorio*, in which he meets Casella, an excellent musician of his time:

> Then he began so sweetly
> That the sweetness still sounds within me [36]

and in his *Paradiso*, in the twenty-third canto:

> Then they remained there in my sight,
> Singing *Regina coeli* so sweetly
> That it has never left my heart [37]

and again in the twenty-seventh canto:

> To Father, Son, and Holy Ghost
> All Paradise took up the Glory
> So that the sweet song intoxicated me. [38]

From these things one may gather that music is pure sweetness and that he who would sing should sing the sweetest music and the sweetest modes well ordered in the sweetest manner.

Beyond this—and this will be the end of my discourse—you will bear in mind that in company a man ought always to be mannerly and courteous, not insisting on his own wishes but yielding to those of others, giving

---

31 1340B (*S.R.* I, 19).

32 *Commentary on the Somnium Scipionis,* II, xxiv, 6.

33 A setting of this poem for four voices by Cipriano da Rore was published in his *Vive fiamme de'vaghi e dilettevoli madrigali* (Venice, 1565).

34 *Rime,* cccxii, 8: *Dolce cantare oneste donne e belle.*

35 *Rime,* cxii, 9: *Qui cantò dolcemente, e qui s'assise.*

36 Lines 113-114:
   Cominciò egli allor sì dolcemente,
   che la dolcezza ancor dentro mi suona.

37 Lines 127-129:
   Indi rimaser lì nel mio cospetto,
   Regina coeli cantando sì dolce,
   che mai da me non si partì il diletto.

38 Lines 1-3:
   Al Padre, al Figlio, allo Spirito Santo
   cominciò Gloria tutto il Paradiso,
   sì che m'inebbriava il dolce canto.

satisfaction to the best of his ability as often as he is called on, not imitating those who always grumble and, if they perform a service, perform it so grudgingly and disagreeably that their compliance becomes a mortification and a burden. Thus your manners will be pleasing and gentle, always at the command of others. When you sing you will take care to stand in a suitable posture, so much like your usual one that your hearers will question whether the sound is coming from your lips or from those of someone else. And you will not imitate those who, with much ado, begin tuning their voices and recounting their misfortunes, saying that they have caught cold, that they have not slept the night before, that their stomach is not right, and other things of this sort, so tedious that before they begin to sing they have canceled the pleasure with their exasperating excuses.

I have come to the end of what I undertook to discuss. May God grant that it may be as helpful and pleasing to you as it was troublesome to me. And I have no doubt at all that it will prove of great service to you if you will be on your guard against those three horrible monsters that prey on virtue—Adulation, Envy, and Ignorance. Of Adulation, Dante says (through the person of Interminelli) in the eighteenth canto of his *Inferno:*

> Down to this have sunk me the flatteries
> Of which my tongue was never weary; [39]

of Envy, gentle Petrarch says:

> O envy, enemy of virtue,
> By nature hostile to fair principles; [40]

and of the Ignorant, Dante sings, in the third canto of his *Inferno,* as follows:

> These have not hope of death,
> And their blind life is so base
> That they are envious of every other fate;
>
> Report of them the world allows not to exist;
> Mercy and Justice disdain them;
> Let us not speak of them, but look and pass. [41]

---

[39] Lines 125–126:
  Quaggiù m'hanno sommerso le lusinghe,
  ond'io non ebbi mai la lingua stucca.

[40] *Rime,* clxxii, 1–2:
  O invidia nimica di vertute,
  Ch'a'bei principii volentier contrasti.

[41] Lines 46–51:

Questi non hanno speranza di morte,
  e lor cieca vita è tanto bassa,
  che invidiosi son d'ogni altra sorte.

Fama di loro il mondo esser non lassa,
  misericordia e giustizia gli sdegna:
  non ragioniam di lor, ma guarda e passa.

12. Vincenzo Galilei

A Florentine nobleman, born circa 1533, Vincenzo was the father of Galileo Galilei, the famous astronomer and philosopher. He was an excellent musician, particularly as a player on the lute and viol, but he is chiefly remembered for the prominent role he played as a member of Bardi's "Camerata," the circle of musicians and amateurs that invented the new *stile recitativo*. Vincenzo's study of ancient Greek music provided him with a basis for his experiments in the new musical style and led to the writing of his *Dialogo della musica antica e della moderna* (1581), in which he attacks the elaborate polyphonic style of the sixteenth century. Galilei died at Florence in 1591.

From the
Dialogo della musica antica e della moderna [1]
[*1581*]

MUSIC was numbered by the ancients among the arts that are called liberal, that is, worthy of a free man, and among the Greeks its masters and discoverers, like those of almost all the other sciences, were always in great esteem. And by the best legislators it was decreed that it must be taught, not only as a lifelong delight but as useful to virtue, to those who were born to acquire perfection and human happiness, which is the object of the state. But in the course of time the Greeks lost the art of music and the other sciences as well, along with their dominion. The Romans had a knowledge of music, obtaining it from the Greeks, but they practiced chiefly that part appropriate to the theaters where tragedy and comedy were performed, without much prizing the part which is concerned with speculation; and being continually engaged in wars, they

---

1 Text: The original edition (Venice, 1581). I have translated pages 80 to 90 and the beginning and end of the dialogue, making a number of cuts. Some of the postils of the original and one parenthesis are given as author's notes.

paid little attention even to the former part and thus easily forgot it. Later, after Italy had for a long period suffered great barbarian invasions, the light of every science was extinguished, and as if all men had been overcome by a heavy lethargy of ignorance, they lived without any desire for learning and took as little notice of music as of the western Indies. And they persisted in this blindness until first Gafurius [2] and after him Glarean and later Zarlino [3] (truly the princes in this modern practice) began to investigate what music was and to seek to rescue it from the darkness in which it had been buried. That part which they understood and appreciated, they brought little by little to its present condition, but from what can be learned from countless passages in the ancient histories and in the poets and philosophers, it does not seem to any who are intelligent that they restored it to its ancient state, or that they attained to the true and perfect knowledge of it. This may have been owing to the rudeness of the times, the difficulty of the subject, and the scarcity of good interpreters.

None the less, these writers deserve the highest praise and the world owes them a perpetual debt; if for nothing else, at least for having given to many the occasion to devote greater labor to the subject, trying to discover how to bring it to perfection. This it seems, but only so far as pertains to theory, has been attained in our times by Girolamo Mei,[4] a man of worth, to whom all musicians and all men should give thanks and honor, and afterwards, in our own city, by the very illustrious Signor Giovanni Bardi de' Conti di Vernio,[5] who having long studied music, and

2 Galilei is presumably referring to the *De harmonia musicorum instrumentorum opus* (Milan, 1518).

3 Although Galilei had been a pupil of Zarlino's in the early sixties and had been in friendly correspondence with Zarlino as late as 1578, his dialogue is essentially a violent attack on the very foundations of Zarlino's teaching. Zarlino replied to this attack in his *Sopplimenti musicali* (Venice, 1588), quoting from his correspondence with Galilei, and Galilei returned to the attack in his *Discorso intorno all'opere di messer Gioseffo Zarlino* (Florence, 1589).

4 Mei is the author of an unpublished treatise on ancient music, *De modis musicis veterum libri quatuor*, the second book of which was published in 1602 in an abridged Italian translation by Pier del Nero. Burney (III, 173, note q) quotes some remarks of Doni's on Galilei's indebtedness to Mei and goes on to say that he has himself examined Mei's MS. In this he discovers "not only opinions similar to those of Galilei, but frequently the words in which they are expressed in his dialogue; particularly in a letter from Mei, dated Rome, 1572, in answer to two that he had received from Galilei, in which he seems to have been consulted concerning the usual difficulties which those have to encounter who undertake

to discuss the music of the ancients. I procured a copy of this letter entire, and considerable extracts from the other writings of Mei, which indeed contain the whole substance of Galilei's dialogue, except the musical scales and proportions of the ancients." It appears very likely that Bardi too owes much to Mei and that some of the similarities between Bardi's *Discorso* and Galilei's *Dialogo* are to be explained in this way. On this question see also Henriette Martin, "Le 'Camerata' du comte Bardi et la musique florentine du XVIe siècle," *Revue de musicologie*, XIII, 63–74, 152–161, 227–234; XIV, 92–100, 141–151.

5 Galilei dedicates his dialogue to Bardi, his "most considerate patron," and in his dedication has this to say about their relationship: "How shall I be able even to begin to repay you for the opportunity that you have given me and that has enabled me to attend with a quiet mind to those studies to which I have devoted myself since my youth and which without your help I should not now have brought to the state in which they are? To this add your readiness to have sent at my instance from the furthest parts of Europe those various books and instruments without which it would have been impossible to acquire that idea of music that by their means we have

finding great delight in it as in all the other sciences, has greatly en-
nobled it and made it worthy of esteem, having by his example incited
the nobles to the same study, many of whom are accustomed to go to
his house and pass the time there in cultivated leisure with delightful
songs and laudable discussions.

Being therefore under great obligation to the courtesy of this most
gracious gentleman, and consequently desiring to show him by some
outward sign my inward wish to serve him, I have judged that I could
not spend the time to better profit than by devoting my energies to this
subject, since I hoped by so doing to give him some sign of gratitude
and to aid the world not a little to escape from the darkness in which it
has been enveloped since the above-mentioned loss. Be this, however, said
without arrogance and with all respect for those who from Guido Aretino
down to our times have written on this subject; although if I should
attribute to myself some little glory in this action, I might perhaps not
merit rebuke, since the inclination for these liberal studies given to me
by nature, and the continual diligence I have employed for many years
in preparing them, would with great reason justify my discussing them.
But let the judgment of this be strictly reserved to those versed in the
subject.

For this reason, apart from the one previously mentioned, and in
order that I may not defraud the world of any benefit it might receive
from my efforts, it has pleased me to publish some thoughts of mine on
ancient music and that of our times, which until this day have been (in
my opinion) little understood by any who have discussed them, a thing
that without further testimony from me may serve as clear evidence of
the difficulty of the subject. I therefore desire of the reader that he be
prepared to pass judgment and to compare my writings with those of
the other moderns with the greatest attention and with his mind free
from any human passion, for it is clear that whoever has not wholly
freed his mind from passion cannot form a perfect judgment of anything. I shall receive with pleasure every suggestion that is given to me
by an understanding man and lover of truth, and shall be obliged to

---

acquired. And so that I might show this science
to the world very much more clearly than, since
its loss, perhaps, it has yet been shown, has it not
seemed to you important to give me opportunity
for travel and to confer on me your favor in
every other necessary matter to seek out many
places and thus to derive further and more accu-
rate ideas from the manners of the inhabitants
and from ancient memoirs and from men versed
in musical science? . . . And what greater sign

of your courtesy and benevolence could you have
given me than often to put to one side your more
serious and important affairs to explain to me
viva voce the obscure meanings of ancient and
important writers, whose ideas, understood by
few, you set so precisely to rights that one would
well have been able to believe that you had found
yourself again in those happy centuries in which
one had the most complete understanding of
music?"

him for it without being ashamed to learn from one who understands better than myself.

And now, since long continuous speaking, flowing on like a torrent, seems not to have that force and vigor in concluding sentences and arguments which dialogue has, I have judged it most to the purpose to treat my present discourses in that manner, and this I can easily believe to have been one of the potent causes that induced Plato to treat the subjects of divine philosophy in this way. I have accordingly chosen to discuss this subject the very illustrious Signor Giovanni Bardi, mentioned a little while ago, and with him Signor Piero Strozzi,[6] as being both most zealous for the true music and great lovers of such speculations as these and moreover qualified to sustain this or even a weightier argument.

. . . . .

(S) May it please you to give me some further particulars, so that I may escape from my ignorance and also learn how to answer the practical musicians of today, who maintain that the music of the ancients was in comparison with their own a thing to be laughed at, and that the astonishment they caused with it in men's minds had no other source or origin than their coarseness and rudeness, but being proud of it, they afterwards made a great to-do over it in their books.

(B) Observe how bold they are, these men who laugh at the effects of a thing without knowing what it was, or what its nature and properties were, or how its effects could have been produced! What better argument do you wish, in order to convince them, than the miracles, to give them that name, that this music performed, miracles related to us by the worthiest and most famous writers, outside the profession of music, that the world has ever had?

But, leaving this to one side, let us turn to a clear and reasonable example, which will be this: from what I have been able to gather, it is certain that the present manner of singing several airs together has not been in use for more than a hundred and fifty years, although I do not know that there exists an authoritative example of the modern practice that is that old or that anyone wishes to have one. And all the best practical musicians agree in saying and believing that between that time and this, music has reached the highest perfection that man can imagine, indeed that since the death of Cipriano Rore, a musician truly unique in

6 Strozzi is also mentioned by Jacopo Peri (*S.R.* III, 15) in connection with his music for *Dafne* and *Euridice*.

this manner of counterpoint, it has rather declined than advanced. Now if in the hundred years, or a little more, that it has been practiced in this manner by people who are commonly of little or no worth, of unknown birthplace and parentage, so to speak, having no gifts of fortune, or else few, and hardly able to read, it has reached the pitch of excellence that they say, how much more astonishing and marvelous it must have been among the Greeks and Romans, where it lasted for centuries and centuries, continually in the care of the wisest, most learned, most judicious, and most wealthy men and of the bravest and most princely commanders that the world has ever had!

．　．　．　．　．

For all the height of excellence of the practical music of the moderns, there is not heard or seen today the slightest sign of its accomplishing what ancient music accomplished, nor do we read that it accomplished it fifty or a hundred years ago when it was not so common and familiar to men. Thus neither its novelty nor its excellence has ever had the power, with our modern musicians, of producing any of the virtuous, infinitely beneficial and comforting effects that ancient music produced. From this it is a necessary conclusion that either music or human nature has changed from its original state. But what ancient music was, and what modern music is, and how this change could come about, this I shall show at the proper time.

(S) I take such pleasure in hearing these novelties which you advocate with such reasonable and living arguments, that if you are content, I shall be glad to hear all that you may wish to say further on the subject and shall not interfere with the order in which you have proposed to yourself to discuss the material.

(B) If that is your pleasure, it shall be mine as well, the more so because, having gone over it in advance, I shall not have to repeat the same thing several times. Let us then determine how much of the proposed material we can truly perceive, without fearing (since our only desire is for the public benefit) any imputation that may be cast on us for having been the first to dare to break this ice, so hard, thick, and plentiful. But observe this: if the practice of music—I mean now the true music which, as Polybius says,[a] is useful to all men, and not that music which, according to Ephorus, was invented to delude and deceive them—if the practice of music, I say, was introduced among men for the reason and

---

a In the preface to his *Histories*. [*Histories*, iv, 20; that part of the passage in question which relates to Ephorus is quoted by Athenaeus, xiv (*S.R.* I, 50).—Ed.]

object that all the learned concur in declaring, namely, if it arose primarily
to express the passions with greater effectiveness in celebrating the praises
of the gods, the genii, and the heroes,[b] and secondarily to communicate
these with equal force to the minds of mortals for their benefit and advantage, then it will be clear that the rules observed by the modern contrapuntists as inviolable laws, as well as those they often use from choice
and to show their learning, will be directly opposed to the perfection
of the true and best harmonies and melodies. It will not be difficult to
prove and demonstrate this to them convincingly, for when they recall
all that has thus far been said on this subject, they will set aside their
own interest and their envy, wrong practice, and ignorance.

As the foundation of this subject, then, I shall briefly mention only
two topics as principal and important, promising to explain them com-
prehensively a little further on. I say accordingly that the nature of the
low sound is one thing, that of the high sound another, and that of the
intermediate sound different from either of these. I say likewise that
fast movement has one property, slow movement another, and that intermediate movement is far from either.[7] Now if these two principles are
true, and they most certainly are, it may easily be gathered from them,
since truth is a unity, that singing in consonance in the manner that the
modern practical musicians use is an absurdity,[c] for consonance is nothing but a mixture of high and low sound which (as you know already)
strikes the ear inoffensively, or delightfully, or very sweetly.

For if we find this contrariety of passion between the extreme sounds
of the simple consonances, how much more the extended and composite
consonances will have, by reason of the greater distance between their
extremes, and how much more than these the consonances that are
several times extended and composite, which because of their greater
distance from their origin are less pure, less perceptible to the ear, and
less comprehensible to the intellect! None the less, the modern practical
musicians go industriously seeking them out on the artificial and natural
instruments. And if the diapason and diapente are as we have described
them, and if the extreme sounds of each of these are perfectly [8] combined, particularly those of the least multiple interval,[d] which because
of their mutual correspondence seem to be almost the same and to unite

---

b Just as the origin of our music for several
voices may be in part comprehended from the
plainsongs of the church.

c To the contrary, Zarlino says in his *Istituzioni*, II, i, xvi, xlix, that harmony is imperfect
without it.

d The diapason.

7 This line of argument is already familiar
from Bardi's *Discorso* (pp. 103-104 above).

8 Galilei writes "separately" (*separatamente*),
which makes little sense in this context; "perfectly" would seem to be required by the se-
quence of his ideas.

in a single term, how much more will the extremes of the imperfect consonances differ in nature, and how much more than these the dissonances of which their music is full! And if such diversity is found between only two parts which together sound a single interval, whether simple or composite, how much greater diversity there will be among four or six or more, often composite and of different natures, sounded together at the same time, as for the most part and to the greater ruin of true music is the custom of the contrapuntists in their *canzoni!*

After these impediments, caused by the diversity of sounds and the variety of voices, those that arise from the unequal movement of the parts are no less important, and these are that the soprano part often hardly moves because of the slowness of its notes, while on the contrary the bass part flies and those of the tenor and alto walk with leisurely pace, or while one of these fairly flies, the bass is proceeding at a walk and the soprano is almost motionless.[9] Thus while the nature of the movement and sound made by one of the parts would be attracting the listener, and the more so when combined with words conforming to this movement and sound, the other part, as its contrary, would be repelling him, not otherwise than would happen to a column, everywhere set evenly upon its base, if anyone, to overthrow it, were to attach two or more equal ropes to its capital, each pulled in an opposite direction from an equal distance with an equal force.[10] For it would not move at all from its place, for all the effort expended, unless perhaps it was somewhat weakened by some imperfection of its own, since the force on one side would counteract the opposite force. But if someone else were to attack it with the same appliances and the same forces, pulling from one side only, it would not be wonderful, to my thinking, if all that effort were strong enough to make it fall.

.   .   .   .   .   .

The present way of composing and singing several airs in consonance at the same time was derived, unless I am mistaken, from stringed instruments similar to the epigonion and the simicion, or from these very ones. Seeing that the strings of these were in their number and arrangement and in the manner of their stretching such as has been shown above, the cithara players of those times began—either for the purpose of somehow surpassing those who sang to the cithara or of escaping the need of

---

9 Cf. Bardi, *Discorso* (pp. 103-104 above); Mei also has this figure: "At the same moment, the soprano scarcely budges while the tenor flies and the bass walks as though with resoled shoes." (I translate the French of Mlle Martin.)

10 Mei also has this figure of the column; cf. the article by Mlle Martin, cited above.

always having a singer with them for the sake of the perfection of the
melody that his voice and their instrument produced—they began, I say,
with that little knowledge of music which they had and with no regard
for the laws of Terpander or of any other approved and authoritative
legislator, to seek a way of somehow delighting the ear with the mere
sound of the instrument, without the aid of the voice. And they decided
that the variety of consonances and harmonies would be an effective
means of coloring this design. Before this time the use of these for the
purpose we have mentioned had not been approved by anyone of sound
mind, but greatly and with just cause abhorred, for it was well known
that consonance had the power of arousing discord in listeners whose
minds were well-ordered.

.   .   .   .   .

Thus the cithara players, wishing to make up for their defect, introduced upon the artificial instruments this way of playing several airs
together in consonance. Long practicing these, and looking always toward
the prescribed end, they began, by long experience, to distinguish in
them what displeased, what caused annoyance, and finally what delighted
the ear. And to have a broader and more spacious field, they introduced
not only the use of imperfect consonances (discreetly so called to make
it seem rather that they were consonances) but also that of dissonances,
seeing that with only the five consonances that the ancients esteemed
(those now called perfect), the matter became tedious and difficult to
manage.

.   .   .   .   .

The practical players of those times therefore began to form, upon
the instruments that I have mentioned to you above, their rules and
laws. The first of these was, that when not more than two strings were
sounded at once, it was forbidden to take, one after another, two of those
consonances that are today called perfect, when these were of the same
species and genus. For this there was no other reason than that with two
strings only, these consonances, because of the simplicity of their extreme
sounds, do not completely delight the ear, for hearing, like all the other
senses, takes pleasure in the diversity of its proper objects. On the other
hand they admitted two and three imperfect consonances as less simple
and more varied, not because of the difference of the major or minor
tone that is found between them, as some make bold to say,[e] but because

e Zarlino, Istituzioni, III, ii.

of the variety of their extremes, which do not blend so well in this respect as those of the perfect consonances. And it is clear that this rule of not taking two or more perfect consonances one after another under the conditions mentioned above was enacted by the legislators only for the situation in which two strings and not more were sounded at the same time, for when three, four, or more strings were sounded upon the artificial instruments, they allowed them, just as they are allowed today, without offense to the ear.

I am well aware that some pedants of our time (I know no politer name to call them by) make bold to say, to those simpler than themselves who listen to them as miracles, that on the keyboard instruments of which they make profession, changing the fingers conceals the two perfect consonances from the sight and not the hearing of those who observe them attentively. Notice, please, what unheard-of folly this is, to wish to make sight a competent judge of the different quality of sounds, which is equivalent to saying that hearing has a share in discerning the differences of colors.

It was from this way of playing in consonance, I say then, that practical musicians, a little before our grandfathers' time, derived the belief that it was also possible to compose and to sing in this manner, for the ancient and learned manner had been lost many, many years before as a result of wars or other circumstances. Of this ancient manner we shall speak a little further on, and we shall throw upon it, in addition to the light we have already thrown, the greatest light possible to our feeble powers, with the sole object of inciting great and virtuous minds to labor in so noble a science and to see to bringing it back to its first and happy state. This I do not consider impossible, knowing that it was not revealed by the stars to those who first discovered it and brought it to the height of perfection, but of a certainty acquired by industrious art and assiduous study. The ancient music, I say, was lost, along with all the liberal arts and sciences, and its light has so dimmed that many consider its wonderful excellence a dream and a fable.

After its loss they began to derive from the stringed and wind instruments and also from the organ, which was in use in those times, although somewhat different from ours, rules and a norm for composing and singing several airs together, just as they had played them on the instruments. And they adopted as laws the same practices that the cithara players and organists had previously been observing, excepting that of not using two perfect consonances of the same species when four or more voices were singing together; perhaps to make the matter more difficult, or to show that they had a more refined and delicate ear than their predecessors, or actually believing that the same conditions which govern the relations of two voices singing together also govern those of four or six or more.

This way of composing and singing, by the novelty which it introduced, along with the ease of quickly becoming a musician, pleased the generality of people, as usually happens, thanks to their imperfection and the little knowledge they always have of what is good and true, and gave opportunities for the artisans to indulge in wild fancies and to introduce further novel doctrines, for the latest comers were unwilling to follow in the footsteps of their predecessors and wholly to approve their work, lest they should seem to be almost confessing by silent consent their inferiority to them in industry and talent; all this with the aim of bringing music to the ruin in which we find it. For this reason they added to the rule that it was permissible to use two imperfect consonances, that these must necessarily be of different species,[11] and further, that in proceeding from imperfect to perfect consonance the progression should always be to the nearest,[12] always meaning in compositions for two voices.

Now you see how, little by little, lured by ambition, they went on without at all perceiving it, making reason subject to sense, the form to the material, the true to the false. Not content with this, men of our time have added to the way of proceeding from imperfect to perfect consonance and from imperfect to imperfect, the rule that one must take into consideration and indeed avoid the relations of the tritone and semidiapente which may arise between the one part and the other,[13] and they have therefore decreed that when a third follows a major sixth, it should always be minor (because the parts have changed position by contrary motion), and that when the major third is followed by a sixth, it should always be minor, and vice versa.[11] They decreed further that when four or more parts are singing together, the lowest part should never be without its third and fifth (or instead of the fifth, the sixth) or one of their extensions.[14]

There is no one who does not consider these rules excellent and necessary for the mere delight the ear takes in the variety of the harmonies, but for the expression of conceptions they are pestilent, being fit for nothing but to make the concentus varied and full, and this is not always,

---

11 Zarlino, *Istituzioni*, III, xxix (pp. 45–48 above).

12 *Ibid.*, III, xxxviii (How we ought to proceed from one consonance to another). The rule in question is of course much older than Zarlino's statement of it, but it is presumably this statement that Galilei has in mind.

13 *Ibid.*, III, xxx (pp. 48–51 above).

14 *Ibid.*, III, xxxi (p. 52 above) and lix.

indeed is never suited to express any conception of the poet or the orator. I repeat, therefore, that if the rules in question had been applied to their original purpose, those who have amplified them in modern times would deserve no less praise than those who first laid them down, but the whole mistake is that the purpose today is different, indeed directly opposed to that of the first inventors of this kind of music, while what the true purpose is has long been evident. It was never the intention of the inventors that these rules should have to serve for the use of those harmonies that, combined with words and with the appropriate passion, express the conceptions of the mind; they were to serve for the sound of the artificial instruments alone, both stringed and wind, as may be gathered from what we have said thus far of their first authors. But the matter has always been understood in the opposite way by their successors, and this belief has endured so long that I think it will be most difficult, if not impossible, to remove and dispel it from men's minds, especially from the minds of those who are mere practitioners of this kind of counterpoint, and therefore esteemed and prized by the vulgar and salaried by various gentlemen, and who have been informing others about this practice, by them called music, down to the present day.

For if anyone wished to persuade such men as these that they were ignorant of the true music, he would need, not the rhetoric of Cicero or Demosthenes, but the sword of the paladin Orlando, or the authority of some great prince who was a friend to truth and who might abandon the vulgar music to the vulgar, as suited to them, and persuade the noble, by his example, to devote themselves to the music suited to them. This is the music that Aristotle calls honest and used with dignity, for in the well-ordered state, as he says in his Eighth Book,[†] those forms of music that are like the vulgar, corrupt and removed from the true form, are conceded to the vulgar, as are those so much admired and prized by them today, for each naturally seeks his like. But of this, enough said.

Consider each rule of the modern contrapuntists by itself, or, if you wish, consider them all together. They aim at nothing but the delight of the ear, if it can truly be called delight. They have not a book among them for their use and convenience that speaks of how to express the conceptions of the mind and of how to impress them with the greatest possible effectiveness on the minds of the listeners; of this they do not think and never have thought since the invention of this kind of music, but only of how to disfigure it still more, if such a thing be possible. And that in truth the last thing the moderns think of is the expression of the

† *Politics*, VIII. [*S.R.* I, 22–23.]

words with the passion that these require, excepting in the ridiculous way that I shall shortly relate, let it be a manifest sign that their observances and rules amount to nothing more than a manner of modulating about among the musical intervals with the aim of making the music a contest of varied harmonies according to the rules stated above and without further thought of the conception and sense of the words. And if it were permitted me, I should like to show you, with several examples of authority, that among the most famous contrapuntists of this century there are some who do not even know how to read, let alone understand. Their ignorance and lack of consideration is one of the most potent reasons why the music of today does not cause in the listeners any of those virtuous and wonderful effects that ancient music caused.

．　．　．　．　．

If the object of the modern practical musicians is, as they say, to delight the sense of hearing with the variety of the consonances, and if this property of tickling (for it cannot with truth be called delight in any other sense) resides in a simple piece of hollow wood over which are stretched four, six, or more strings of the gut of a dumb beast or of some other material, disposed according to the nature of the harmonic numbers, or in a given number of natural reeds or of artificial ones made of wood, metal, or some other material, divided by proportioned and suitable measures, with a little air blowing inside them while they are touched or struck by the clumsy and untutored hand of some base idiot or other, then let this object of delighting with the variety of their harmonies be abandoned to these instruments, for being without sense, movement, intellect, speech, discourse, reason, or soul, they are capable of nothing else. But let men, who have been endowed by nature with all these noble and excellent parts, endeavor to use them not merely to delight, but as imitators of the good ancients, to improve at the same time, for they have the capacity to do this and in doing otherwise they are acting contrary to nature, which is the handmaiden of God.

Judicious and learned men, when they regard the various colors and shapes of objects, do not find satisfaction, like the ignorant multitude, in the mere pleasure that sight affords, but in investigating afterwards the mutual appropriateness and proportion of these incidental attributes and likewise their properties and nature. In the same way, I say that it is not enough merely to take pleasure in the various harmonies heard between the parts of a musical composition unless one also determines the proportion in which the voices are combined, in order not to be like the herbalist who in his simplicity knows nothing about simples except their names—and such are most of those who pass for musicians today among the vulgar.

Among their absurdities and novelties is also numbered that of sometimes transposing music originally composed according to natural, singable, and usual movements up or down to strange pitches that are unsingable, altogether out of the ordinary, and full of artifice (just as skilled organists are accustomed to transpose for the convenience of the chorus, using accidental signs, by a tone, a third, or some other interval), and this only in order to vaunt themselves and their achievements as miracles before those more ignorant than themselves. Add to this that among the more famous there are and always have been those who have first put notes together according to their caprice and have then fitted to them whatever words they pleased, not minding at all that there was the same incongruity between the words and their notes as that which has been said to exist between the dithyramb and the Dorian harmony,[15] or a greater one, for even men of worth are amazed that most modern compositions sound better when well played than when well sung, failing to perceive that their purpose is to be communicated to the hearer by means of artificial instruments and not of natural ones, since they are artifice itself and not at all natural. And to diminish still further their amazement and my trouble in so often reciting the words of others, let them read in this connection the tenth problem in Aristotle's Nineteenth Book,[16] which will dispose of them.

Beyond the beauty and grace of the consonances, there is nothing ingenious or choice in modern counterpoint excepting the use of the dissonances, provided these are arranged with the necessary means and judiciously resolved. For the expression of conceptions in order to impress the passions on the listener, both of them are not merely a great impediment, but the worst of poisons. The reason is this: the continual sweetness of the various harmonies, combined with the slight harshness and bitterness of the various dissonances (besides the thousand other sorts of artifice that the contrapuntists of our day have so industriously sought out to allure our ears, to enumerate which I omit lest I become tedious), these are, as I have said, the greatest impediment to moving the mind to any passion. For the mind, being chiefly taken up and, so to speak, bound by the snares of the pleasure thus produced, is not given time to under-

---

15 Aristotle, *Politics*, 1342B (*S.R.* I, 23).

16 "Why is it that—granting that the human voice is a pleasanter sound than that of instru-ments—the voice of one who sings without words—as do those who hum—is not so pleasant as the sound of aulos or lyre?" [Hett].

stand, let alone consider, the badly uttered words. All this is wholly different from what is necessary to passion from its nature, for passion and moral character must be simple and natural, or at least appear so, and their sole aim must be to arouse their counterpart in others.

(S) From what you have said thus far may be gathered, it seems, among other important things, that the music of today is not of great value for expressing the passions of the mind by means of words, but is of value merely for the wind and stringed instruments, from which the ear, it appears, desires nothing but the sweet enjoyment of the variety of their harmonies, combined with the suitable and proportioned movements of which they have an abundance; these are then made manifest to the ear by some practiced and skilled performer.

(B) What you say would always be the case if the various harmonies of the artificial instruments were fit only to divert and tickle the ears, as you say, and if the contrapuntists of our time were content to disfigure only the part of music that pertains to the expression of conceptions. But they have not been content with this and have treated no better the part having to do with the harmonies of the artificial instruments in themselves and concerned with the pleasure of the sense without going on to that of the mind. This too they have reduced to such estate that if it were to get the least bit worse, it would need rather to be buried than to be cured.

. . . . . .

Finally I come as I promised to the treatment of the most important and principal part of music, the imitation of the conceptions that are derived from the words. After disposing of this question I shall speak to you about the principles observed by the ancient musicians.

Our practical contrapuntists say, or rather hold to be certain, that they have expressed the conceptions of the mind in the proper manner and have imitated the words whenever, in setting to music a sonnet, *canzone, romanzo*, madrigal, or other poem in which there occurs a line saying, for example:

Bitter heart and savage, and cruel will,[17]

which is the first line of one of the sonnets of Petrarch, they have caused many sevenths, fourths, seconds, and major sixths to be sung between the

---

17 Petrarch, *Rime*, cclxv, 1: *Aspro core e selvaggio, e cruda voglia;* it will be recalled that Willaert's setting of this poem was cited by Zarlino in his *Institutions*, IV, xxxii (p. 68 above) as a model of correct musical expression.

parts and by means of these have made a rough, harsh, and unpleasant sound in the ears of the listeners.[g]

The sound is indeed not unlike that given by the cithara of Orpheus in the hands of Neantius, the son of Pittacus, the tyrant of the Greek island of Lesbos, where flourished the greatest and most esteemed musicians of the world, in honor of whose greatness it had been deposited there, we read, after the death of the remarkable cithara player Pericletus, the glorious winner in the Carneian festival of the Lacedaemonians. When this Neantius played upon the cithara in question, it was revealed by his lack of skill that the strings were partly of wolf-gut and partly of lamb-gut, and because of this imperfection [h]—or because of the transgression he had committed in taking the sacred cithara from the temple by deceit, believing that the virtue of playing it well resided in it by magic, as in Bradamante's lance that of throwing to the ground whomsoever she touched with it [18]—he received, when he played it, condign punishment, being devoured by dogs. This was his only resemblance to the learned poet, sage priest, and unique musician who as you know was slain by the Bacchantes.

At another time they will say that they are imitating the words when among the conceptions of these there are any meaning "to flee" or "to fly"; these they will declaim with the greatest rapidity and the least grace imaginable. In connection with words meaning "to disappear," "to swoon," "to die," or actually "to be extinct" they have made the parts break off so abruptly, that instead of inducing the passion corresponding to any of these, they have aroused laughter and at other times contempt in the listeners, who felt that they were being ridiculed. Then with words meaning "alone," "two," or "together" they have caused one lone part, or two, or all the parts together to sing with unheard-of elegance. Others, in the singing of this particular line from one of the sestinas of Petrarch:

And with the lame ox he will be pursuing Laura,[19]

have declaimed it to staggering, wavering, syncopated notes as though they had the hiccups. And when, as sometimes happens, the conceptions they have had in hand made mention of the rolling of the drum, or of the sound of the trumpet or any other such instrument, they have sought to represent its sound in their music, without minding at all that they

---

g Zarlino, *Istituzioni*, III, lxvi, IV, xxxii. [Page 67 above.]

h Fracastoro, *De antipathia et sympathia rerum*, i.

18 Ariosto, *Orlando furioso*, VIII, xvii; XXX, xv.

19 *Rime*, ccxxxix, 36: *E col bue zoppo andrem cacciando l'aura* (Galilei writes *andrà* and *Laura*). Cf. the setting of this line by Orlando di Lasso (*Sämmtliche Werke*, IV, 80).

were pronouncing these words in some unheard-of manner. Finding words denoting diversity of color, such as "dark" or "light" hair and similar expressions, they have put black or white notes beneath them to express this sort of conception craftily and gracefully, as they say, meanwhile making the sense of hearing subject to the accidents of color and shape, the particular objects of sight and, in solid bodies, of touch. Nor has there been any lack of those who, still more corrupt, have sought to portray with notes the words "azure" and "violet" according to their sound, just as the stringmakers nowadays color their gut strings. At another time, finding the line:

He descended into hell, into the lap of Pluto,

they have made one part of the composition descend in such a way that the singer has sounded more like someone groaning to frighten children and terrify them than like anyone singing sense. In the opposite way, finding this one:

This one aspires to the stars,

in declaiming it they have ascended to a height that no one shrieking from excessive pain, internal or external, has ever reached. And coming, as sometimes happens, to words meaning "weep," "laugh," "sing," "shout," "shriek," or to "false deceits," "harsh chains," "hard bonds," "rugged mount," "unyielding rock," "cruel woman," and the like, to say nothing of their sighs, unusual forms, and so on, they have declaimed them, to color their absurd and vain designs, in manners more outlandish than those of any far-off barbarian.

Unhappy men, they do not perceive that if Isocrates or Corax or any of the other famous orators had ever, in an oration, uttered two of these words in such a fashion, they would have moved all their hearers to laughter and contempt and would besides this have been derided and despised by them as men foolish, abject, and worthless. And yet they wonder that the music of their times produces none of the notable effects that ancient music produced, when, quite the other way, they would have more cause for amazement if it were to produce any of them, seeing that their music is so remote from the ancient music and so unlike it as actually to be its contrary and its mortal enemy, as has been said and proved and will be proved still more, and seeing that it has no means enabling it even to think of producing such effects, let alone to obtain them. For its sole aim is to delight the ear, while that of ancient music is to induce in another the same passion that one feels oneself. No person of judgment understands the expression of the conceptions of the mind by means of words in this ridiculous manner, but in another, far removed and very different.

(S) I pray you, tell me how.

(B) In the same way that, among many others, those two famous orators that I mentioned a little while ago expressed them, and afterwards every musician of repute. And if they wish to understand the manner of it, I shall content myself with showing them how and from whom they can learn with little pain and trouble and with the greatest pleasure, and it will be thus: when they go for their amusement to the tragedies and comedies that the mummers act, let them a few times leave off their immoderate laughing, and instead be so good as to observe, when one quiet gentleman speaks with another, in what manner he speaks, how high or low his voice is pitched, with what volume of sound, with what sort of accents and gestures, and with what rapidity or slowness his words are uttered. Let them mark a little what difference obtains in all these things when one of them speaks with one of his servants, or one of these with another; let them observe the prince when he chances to be conversing with one of his subjects and vassals; when with the petitioner who is entreating his favor; how the man infuriated or excited speaks; the married woman, the girl, the mere child, the clever harlot, the lover speaking to his mistress as he seeks to persuade her to grant his wishes, the man who laments, the one who cries out, the timid man, and the man exultant with joy. From these variations of circumstance, if they observe them attentively and examine them with care, they will be able to select the norm of what is fitting for the expression of any other conception whatever that can call for their handling.[20]

Every brute beast has the natural faculty of communicating its pleasure and its pain of body and mind, at least to those of its own species, nor was voice given to them by nature for any other purpose. And among rational animals there are some so stupid that, since they do not know, thanks to their worthlessness, how to make practical application of this faculty and how to profit by it on occasion, they believe that they are without it naturally.[21]

---

20 "*O bel discorso*, truly worthy of the great man he imagines himself to be! From it we may gather that what he actually wishes is to reduce music greatly in dignity and reputation, when, to learn imitation, he bids us go to hear the zanies in tragedies and comedies and to become out-and-out actors and buffoons. What has the musician to do with those who recite tragedies and comedies?" (Zarlino, *Sopplimenti*, VIII, xi).

21 "Thus in his opinion it is a shameful thing to be more man than beast, or at least to be more the modest man than the buffoon, because at the right time and place the songs of the buffoon may move his listeners to laughter. It is not perceived that such imitations belong rather to the orator than to the musician and that when the singer uses such means, he ought rather to be called an actor or a buffoon, than a singer. Everyone knows that the orator who wishes to move

When the ancient musician sang any poem whatever, he first considered very diligently the character of the person speaking: his age, his
sex, with whom he was speaking, and the effect he sought to produce
by this means; and these conceptions, previously clothed by the poet
in chosen words suited to such a need, the musician then expressed in the
tone [22] and with the accents and gestures, the quantity and quality of
sound, and the rhythm appropriate to that action and to such a person.
For this reason we read of Timotheus, who in the opinion of Suidas was
a player of the aulos and not of the cithara,[23] that when he roused the
great Alexander with the difficult mode of Minerva to combat with the
armies of his foes, not only did the circumstances mentioned reveal
themselves in the rhythms, the words, and the conceptions of the entire
song in conformity with his desire, but in my opinion at least, his habit,
the aspect of his countenance, and each particular gesture and member
must have shown on this occasion that he was burning with desire to
fight, to overcome, and to conquer the enemy. For this reason Alexander
was forced to cry out for his arms and to say that this should be the
song of kings.[24] And rightly, for provided the impediments have been
removed, if the musician has not the power to direct the minds of his
listeners to their benefit, his science and knowledge are to be reputed null
and vain, since the art of music was instituted and numbered among the
liberal arts for no other purpose.

.   .   .   .   .   .

(S) I have only one remaining doubt, Signor Giovanni, which by
your leave will serve as a seal for our discussion, and it is this: how does
it happen that the compositions of many who are generally reputed to
be great players, both of the lute and of the keyboard instruments, do
not succeed when they play them on these instruments, and that other
players, also of repute, have left no other memory than their names?
And that on the other hand there are some of little repute with the general
public who have succeeded excellently in writing in their chosen profes-

---

the passions must study them and must imitate
not only the actor but any other sort of person
who might help him to this end. This the great
orator Cicero did, practicing continually with
the actor Roscius and the poet Architus. But in
this case, what becomes the orator does not become the musician." (Zarlino, *Sopplimenti,*
VIII, xi).

22 Galilei is using the word "tone" (*tono*) in
its technical sense.

23 *Lexicon,* under Timotheus: "When on one
occasion Timotheus the aulos-player played on
the aulos the nome of Athena called Orthios,
they say that Alexander was so moved that, as

he listened, he sprang to arms and said that
this should be the royal aulos-music."

24 "So that this Timotheus of his ought, if not
to be, at least to seem the most perfect of zanies
and buffoons. But who ever heard finer or sweeter
discourse than this, all stuff and nonsense?
Thus, leaving the *zanni,* the *zannini,* and the
zannoli to one side, we shall now explain how
one ought to speak in an imitation made by
means of music" (Zarlino, *Sopplimenti,* VIII,
xi). Zarlino goes on to a discussion of the references to music at the beginning of Aristotle's
Poetics.

sion? And that other musicians are very learned and erudite, and for all that, on the practical side, their compositions have not been at all satisfactory when performed? And that others will hardly know how to read, and will have very little knowledge of practical matters, especially in music, and for all that they will succeed marvelously in counterpoint? And finally, which of these are to be more reputed and esteemed, and which less, and why?

(B) Properly to clear up your doubts, I should need your permission to speak freely (for at the beginning of our discussion you said that this befitted those who seek the truth of things), but since according to the flatterers of today it is ill-bred to name anyone and reproach him with reason in order that he may learn his error and mend his ways, I shall go over them in whatever random order occurs to me and say what I think of them with the greatest modesty at my command, not because what could be said of any is not pure truth, but in order not to be considered slanderous (even with complete injustice) by the envious and malicious.

I say then that in our times there have been and are many excellent players, both of the lute and of the keyboard instruments, among whom some have indeed known how to play well and how to write well, or let us say how to compose well, for their instrument, as for the keyboard instrument an Annibale Padovano and for the lute a Fabrizio Dentice, noble Neapolitan.

Others there have been and are who . . . will know how to write and to show their knowledge excellently and who will observe every slightest particular detail that is needed for good playing and good composition, but apart from this the imagination of one is so lacking in invention, and the fingers and hands of another, either from some natural defect, or from having exercised them little, or from some other circumstance, are so weak or so unskilled in obeying the commands given to them by reason, that he is unable to express the passions with them as he understands them and has engraved them in his thought; these are the reasons why neither the one nor the other gives entire satisfaction in what he does and why they give up the attempt, still seeking, like the orator, to remedy this defect with the pen, with which some of them have been remarkably successful.

Others there have been and are who will play well on one or the other instrument and yet will write badly. Of these a part, being more prudent, have never taken the pains to show their knowledge to the world with the pen, and if they have composed or written anything, have not published it, well aware that it was of little or no worth and that it would thus have brought discredit on them if it had come into the hands of this or that man of understanding.

There are others who have not known how to do the one thing or the other; none the less they have been and are reputed by many to be men of worth. And the same thing that has happened to players has likewise happened (as you will understand) to simple contrapuntists.

.   .   .   .   .

As to which of all these sorts of men deserve to be more esteemed than others, I think that one may safely say that those who play, compose, and likewise write excellently not only merit the highest praise, but deserve to be greatly esteemed and prized by every man of sound intellect.

Those who are more learned than these are no less deserving, although they may be less favored by nature in ready liveliness of hand and in contrapuntal invention, no less deserving, that is, when their knowledge not only makes up for this deficiency but exceeds that of the first sort. For those who teach us a virtue are much more to be esteemed, and the rarer and more excellent they are the more so, than those who merely delight us with their buffooneries; first because it is a greater and a higher thing to know what another does than to do what he does, and then because every purely sensual pleasure ends by satiating us (by reason of its inconstancy) and never makes us thirst for any knowledge. And I say that they are even more deserving when that knowledge of theirs is combined with the highest character, as these are the things chiefly to be desired in the perfect musician and in every follower of the arts, in order that with his learning and his character he may make those who frequent him and listen to him men of learning and good character. In addition I say that it is impossible to find a man who is truly a musician and is vicious, and that if a man has a vicious nature, it will be difficult, or rather impossible for him to be virtuous and to make others virtuous. And to say even more, the man who has in his boyhood used every necessary means and proper care to learn the science of the true music, devoting to it all his labor and effort, will praise and embrace everything that accords with dignity and honesty and will denounce and flee from the contrary, and he will be the last to commit any ugly or unseemly action, and gathering from music most copious fruits, he will be of infinite advantage and utility

1 Plutarch. *De musica*, xli.

both to himself and to his state, nor will he ever, in any place or at any time, do or say any inconsiderate thing, but will continually be guided by decorum, modesty, and reverence.

I turn to those of the third circle and say that they should and can content themselves with being somewhat esteemed by persons who are inferior to them in knowledge. Their worth may be compared to the singing of boys, who are praised and caressed by everyone so long as they have their beautiful voices and throats, but when from any incidental cause their organ is impaired by losing or temporarily losing that little grace, beauty, and sonority of voice, they lose at the same time all their credit, reputation, and skill. None the less, whoever well considers it cannot deny the skill, nor can he deny the hoarseness and the change of voice. And the skill of these is like the fleeting beauty of woman, who, as long as her face retains that desirable disposition of lineaments and colors that combine to form its beauty, is admired by all the world, not for being learned or intelligent in some art or science, but for being beautiful because of the harmony of these incidental details. As these lineaments begin to be altered and cease to preserve that perfect proportion which formerly existed among them, that beauty withers like a garden flower.

With this conclusion, then, the most illustrious Signor Giovanni Bardi, a rare example of every royal virtue, gave his discourse an end.

13. G. P. da Palestrina

Giovanni Pierluigi da Palestrina was born about 1525 at Palestrina, not far from Rome. At first he occupied the position of organist and choirmaster in his native town; in later life he became *magister puerorum* at the Cappella Giulia in Rome. As a young man he sang in the choir of the Sistine Chapel, but after the death of Pope Marcellus II he was removed from this position. In 1555 Palestrina was appointed choirmaster at S. Giovanni in Laterano. In 1561 he exchanged this position with a similar one at S. Maria Maggiore, where he remained until 1571. Palestrina died at Rome in 1594.

Motettorum liber quartus [1]

[Rome, 1584]

Dedication

To Our Most Holy Lord Gregory XIII, Supreme Pontiff:

There are too many poems with no other subject matter than loves alien to the Christian profession and name. These poems, written by men truly carried away by fury, corrupters of youth, a great many musicians have chosen as the material for their skill and industry, and while they have been distinguished by the praise of their talent, they have equally given offense to good and serious men. I blush and grieve to admit that I was once one of their number. But now, when past things cannot be changed and things done cannot be undone, I have changed my purpose. Therefore I have both already labored on those poems which have been written of the praises of our Lord Jesus Christ and his Most Holy Mother the Virgin Mary,[2] and at this time chosen those

---

1 Text: *Werke*, IV (Leipzig, 1874), v.
2 A reference to his first book of spiritual madrigals, published in 1581 (*Werke*, XXIX [Leipzig, 1883], 1–92) and dedicated to Giacomo Boncompagni, Gregory's natural son.

which contain the divine love of Christ and his spouse the soul, indeed the Canticles of Solomon. I have used a kind of music somewhat livelier than I have been accustomed to use in ecclesiastical melodies, for this I felt that the subject itself demanded. It has been my wish, indeed, to offer this work, such as it is, to Your Holiness, who I doubt not will certainly be satisfied by the intent and the endeavor, if less so by the thing itself. But if (may it so befall!) I shall give satisfaction with the thing itself, I shall be encouraged to produce others which I shall expect to please Your Holiness. May God, as long as may be, preserve for us Gregory, the most vigilant shepherd, with the greatest love for his flock, and heap all felicity upon him.

His humble servant,
Giovanni Aloysio Palestrina.

14. Orlando di Lasso

Born at Mons in Belgium circa 1532, Di Lasso went as a boy to Sicily and Milan, where he stayed until 1550. From there he moved on to Naples and then to Rome, where he can be traced in 1553. A trip through France and England ended in Antwerp. In 1556 Di Lasso entered the service of Duke Albrecht V of Bavaria and in 1560 he was appointed choirmaster to the Bavarian court, a position he retained until his death, which occurred in 1594.

Cantiones sacrae [1]

[*1593*]

Dedication

To the Most Reverend and Illustrious Prince and Lord, Lord Johann Otto, Bishop of Augsburg, his very benevolent lord and patron

MOST THINGS in this universe so differ in men's judgments that some give more pleasure shortly after they have come into being and, as it were, while still in their vernal flower, others when they have grown to maturity, but none, or surely very few, gain favor when they are already failing and threaten to pass away. It is thus with the mastery of our harmonic art, music. In this age of annually renewed fertility, abounding in *cantiones* of every kind and in rival composers who daily come forward with the desire of pleasing, nay of winning for themselves the foremost place, it seems not easy to determine whether this divine art has attained its full growth, not to say the peak, the summit of its perfection, or whether it is decking itself with flowers after a new birth. Indeed, if we rely solely on the judgment of our senses, disregarding the counsel of reason, then arbors covered with new vines, ornamented

1 Text: *Sämmtliche Werke*, XIII (Leipzig, 1901), vii–viii.

with a luxuriant growth of shoots and tendrils, are more pleasing to the eye than old vines, set out in rows and tied to stakes and props, but with their stocks roughened and split open by age. Yet the first are virtually unfruitful, while the second yield a liquor which is most sweet to mankind, rejecting all that is useless. In the same way, in estimating the *cantiones* which I composed long ago, in the springtime of my life and the ardor of my years, and those which I produce now, in my old age, I have come to think that while the former are more likely to please, because they are more gay and festive, the latter reveal in their sound more substance and energy, and afford a profounder pleasure to the mind and the ear of the critic. Let the impartial auditor consider whether my measures, soon to withdraw from the theater of this world, are not like the light of day, which is wont to be sweeter just before sunset:

> *Ut esse Phoebi dulcius lumen solet*
> *Jam jam cadentis.*

Intending therefore to publish the present collection of *cantiones*, called motets, written for six voices, a venerable if less melodious music, I had need to seek a patron of sacred and distinguished name, to whom in accordance with my earnest desire, I might consecrate them. I immediately found you, Most Illustrious and Eminent Johann, Most Reverend Prince, being moved to this primarily by my admiration of your manifold and splendid virtues, especially directed toward men of my profession, and of the extreme inclination and liberality of your mind to this same art, and being moreover confident that your Most Reverend Eminence will receive with kindly and cheerful countenance and with attentive ears this music of Orlandus, perhaps my swan song, and would not reject the composer, who most humbly commends himself to you.

Munich, on the feast-day of Michael the Archangel
In the year 1593

To the Most Reverend, Illustrious, and Eminent
Johann

Most respectfully
Orlandus Lassus, Choirmaster to the Most
Serene Duke of Bavaria

15. William Byrd

Born in 1543, William Byrd died at Stondon, Essex, in 1623. A pupil of Thomas Tallis, he was appointed organist of Lincoln Cathedral in 1563, and in 1570 was sworn in as a member of the Chapel Royal. There he shared with Tallis the honorary post of organist. Byrd remained a Catholic throughout his life, as shown in his will, dated 1622.

Byrd is perhaps the most outstanding Elizabethan composer of sacred music and one of the chief writers for the virginals. Among his works are the two books of the *Gradualia,* the dedications and forewords of which are given below. Byrd's virginal pieces are preserved in many manuscript collections of English keyboard music. In the Fitzwilliam Virginal Book alone he is represented with seventy pieces.

Gradualia [1]

[1605–1607]

Dedications and forewords

To that Most Illustrious and Distinguished Man, and his Right Honorable Lord, Henry Howard, Earl of Northampton, Warden of the Cinque Ports, and one of the Privy Council of His Most Serene Majesty, James, King of Great Britain

THE SWAN, they say, when his death is near, sings more sweetly. However little I may be able to attain to the sweetness of that bird in these songs which I have judged should be dedicated to you, most illustrious Henry, I have had two defences or incentives of no common rate for emulating that sweetness in some sort at least. The one was the sweetness of the words themselves, the other your worthiness. For even as

1 Text: *Tudor Church Music,* VII (Oxford, 1927), facs. before pp. 3 and 209.

among artisans it is shameful in a craftsman to make a rude piece of work from some precious material, so indeed to sacred words in which the praises of God and of the Heavenly host are sung, none but some celestial harmony (so far as our powers avail) will be proper. Moreover in these words, as I have learned by trial, there is such a profound and hidden power that to one thinking upon things divine and diligently and earnestly pondering them, all the fittest numbers occur as if of themselves and freely offer themselves to the mind which is not indolent or inert. Truly your worthiness is as great as that of your most ancient family, which, long beaten by bitter storms and stricken, as it were, by the frost of adverse fortune, now in part flourishes again in your own person, and in part, encouraged by the King's Most Serene Majesty, sends out, by your labor and merits, rays of its ancient splendor to the eager eyes of all Englishmen. Since you are also of the King's Privy Council, you always suggest, always further, those things which tend to the greater glory of God, to the greatness of this entire realm, now happily united under one sovereign, James, and most particularly to the honorable tranquillity and peace of all honest private men. In these things the praise due to you is the greater for that in their accomplishment you direct and aim all your efforts, not at popular favor, which you deem vain, nor at the desire of gain, which you consider base, but to the honor only of God, who sees in dark places. And these matters are indeed public, and truly honorable, such as not merely by any songs of mine, but by the mouth and pen of all, will be transmitted to our posterity and to foreign nations, among whom your name is renowned.

But private reasons also impelled me to use my utmost industry in this matter. I have had and still have you, if I err not, as a most benevolent patron in the distressed affairs of my family. You have often listened with pleasure to my melodies, which from men like yourself is a reward to musicians and, so to speak, their highest honorarium. At your plea and request, the Most Serene King has augmented me and my fellows who serve His Majesty's person in music with new benefits and with increases of stipend. For this reason I have resolved that this work of mine (if by chance it shall be of such desert) shall stand as an everlasting testimony of the gratitude of all our hearts to His Majesty and to yourself, distinguished patron, and of my affectionate wishes for those eminent men, whom I love and honor as I perform this office for them. You see, Right Honorable Earl, with what defenders I am provided and by what incentives I am prompted in wishing (if only I could) to imitate the swan.

With truly excellent judgment Alexander forbade any but Apelles

or Lysippus to paint him or to sculpture him in bronze. Nor has it been
in any way granted to me to satisfy my task, save only that I have tried
to ornament things divine with the highest art at my command and to
offer nothing not wrought with care to so distinguished a man as yourself. If I have accomplished this, I shall declare these lucubrations of
mine (for so without falsehood I may call the products of nightly toil)
my swan songs. This they will surely be, if not for their sweetness, at
least as proceeding from such age. While I indeed decided at the request of friends to work upon them and to spread them abroad, it was
you alone that I set before me in my mind as shining above me like a
star guiding me on a course beset with rocks. If in your judgment I
have brought back wares not wholly without use, it will be the unique con-
solation of my old age to have brought into the light a work not unmeet
for our Most Serene King, whose honor I have wished to augment in
my epistle, nor for you, most generous Lord, skilled in the knowledge
of human and divine letters, nor unworthy of my years, which I have
all consumed in music. Farewell.

To your most Worshipful Honor,
William Byrd.

The Author
To the True Lovers of Music

For you, most high-minded and righteous, who delight at times to
sing to God in hymns and spiritual songs, are here set forth for your
exercising the Offices for the whole year which are proper to the chief
Feasts of the Blessed Virgin Mary and of All Saints; moreover others
in five voices with their words drawn from the fountain of Holy Writ;
also the Office at the Feast of Corpus Christi, with the more customary
antiphons of the same Blessed Virgin and other songs in four voices of
the same kind; also all the hymns composed in honor of the Virgin;
finally, various songs in three voices sung at the Feast of Easter. Further,
to the end that they may be ordered each in its own place in the various
parts of the service, I have added a special index at the end of the book;
here all that are proper to the same feasts may easily be found grouped
together, though differing in the number of voices.

If to these pious words I have set notes not unfitting (as I have wished
and as they require), may the honor, as is just, be to God and the pleasure
be yours. Howsoever this may be, give them fair and friendly judgment, and commend me to God in your prayers. Farewell.

To the Right Illustrious and Honorable
John Lord Petre of Writtle, his
most clement Maecenas,
Salutation

Since I have attained to such length of years, relying upon the divine
mercy, that I have seen many of my pupils in music, men indeed peculiarly
skillful in that art, finish their allotted time while I survived, and since
also in my own house I consider that the benefits of the divine bounty
have been directed toward me, indeed have been showered upon me,
my mind is eager, remembering my faith, duty, and piety to God, to
leave to posterity a public testimony, at least in some sort, of a heart
grateful and referring all things, if this be counted a merit, to my
Creator. Having attained to this age, I have attempted, out of devotion
to the divine worship, myself unworthy and unequal, to affix notes, to
serve as a garland, to certain pious and honeyed praises of the Christian
rite to be sung by four, five, or six voices. These are adapted to the
glorious Nativity of Christ our Savior, the Epiphany, the Resurrection,
and finally to the Feast of Saints Peter and Paul.

These songs, most Christian Sir, long since completed by me and
committed to the press, should in my judgment be dedicated to you above
all others, for you are held renowned for the harmony of virtues and
letters and distinguished by your love for all the daughters of the
Muses and of science. Inasmuch as these musical lucubrations, like fruits
sprung from a fertile soil, have mostly proceeded from your house (truly
most friendly to me and mine), and from that tempering of the sky have
brought forth more grateful and abundant fruits, receive, then, Right
Honorable Lord, these little flowers, plucked as it were from your gar-
dens and most rightfully due to you as tithes, and may it be no burden
to you to protect these my last labors, to the end that they may go forth
to the public under the auspices of your most renowned name, to the
glory of God the Greatest and Best, to the greatness of your honor, and
finally for the pleasure of all who properly cultivate the Muses. Meanwhile I pray from my soul that all present things may be of good omen
to you and all future things happy. Farewell.

The third day of April in the year of man's salvation restored 1607.

Your Honor's most dutiful
William Byrde.

16. Henry Peacham

Born circa 1576, Henry Peacham settled in London in 1612 and spent the years 1613–14 traveling in France, Italy, Westphalia, and the Netherlands. He had many friends in musical circles, among them the lutenist and composer John Dowland. His most important book, *The Compleat Gentleman*, appeared in 1622 and was reissued in 1626 and 1627. Peacham was an ardent supporter of the royal cause, but his book teaches a more or less Puritan concept of duty. Thus *The Compleat Gentleman* may be called an English Puritan counterpart to Castiglione's *Cortegiano*. Peacham's last book was published in 1642, and he died soon thereafter.

From The Compleat Gentleman [1]

[*1622*]

OF MUSIC

Music, a sister to Poetry, next craveth your acquaintance, if your genius be so disposed. I know there are many who are *adeo ἄμουσοι* and of such disproportioned spirits that they avoid her company (as a great cardinal in Rome did roses at their first coming in, that to avoid their scent he built him an house in the champaign [*campagna*], far from any town) or, as with a rose not long since, a great lady's cheek in England, their ears are ready to blister at the tenderest touch thereof. I dare not pass so rash a censure of these as Pindar doth,[2] or the Italian, having fitted a proverb to the same effect, "Whom God loves not, that man loves not music"; but I am verily persuaded they are by nature very ill disposed and of such a brutish stupidity that scarce anything else that is good

---

1 Text: The Clarendon Press reprint of the edition of 1634 (Oxford, 1906), pp. 96–104. I have printed some of the postils of the original as author's notes. *The Compleat Gentleman* was first published in 1622.

2 Pythian Odes, I, 13–14: But all the beings that Zeus hath not loved, are astonished, when they hear the voice of the Pierides, whether on the earth, or on the resistless sea. [Sandys]

and savoreth of virtue is to be found in them. Never wise man, I think, questioned the lawful use hereof, since it is an immediate gift of heaven, bestowed on man, whereby to praise and magnify his Creator; to solace him in the midst of so many sorrows and cares, wherewith life is hourly beset; and that by song, as by letters, the memory of doctrine and the benefits of God might be forever preserved (as we are taught by that song of Moses [a] and those divine psalms of the sweet singer of Israel, who with his psaltery [b] so loudly resounded the mysteries and innumerable benefits of the Almighty Creator) and the service of God advanced (as we may find in 2 Samuel vi:5, Psalm 33, 21, 43, and 4, 108, 3,[3] and in sundry other places of scripture which for brevity I omit).

But, say our sectaries, the service of God is nothing advanced by singing and instruments as we use it in our cathedral churches, that is, by "antiphony,[c] rests, repetitions, variety of moods and proportions, with the like."

For the first, that it is not contrary but consonant to the word of God so in singing to answer either, the practice of Miriam, the prophetess and sister of Moses, when she answered the men in her song,[4] will approve; for repetition, nothing was more usual in the singing of the Levites, and among the psalms of David the 136th is wholly compounded of those two most graceful and sweet figures of repetition, symploce and anaphora. For resting and proportions, the nature of the Hebrew verse, as the meanest Hebrician knoweth, consisting many times of uneven feet, going sometime in this number, sometimes in that (one while, as St. Jerome saith,[5] in the numbers of Sappho, another while, of Alcaeus), doth of necessity require it. And wherein doth our practice of singing and playing with instruments in his Majesty's chapel and our cathedral churches differ from the practice of David, the priests, and Levites? [d] Do we not make one sign in praising and thanking God with voices and instruments of all sorts? "Donec," as St. Jerome saith,[6] "reboet laquear templi"; the roof of the church echoeth again, and which, lest they should cavil at as a Jewish ceremony, we know to have been practiced in the ancient purity of the church. But we return where we left.

The physicians will tell you that the exercise of music is a great lengthener of the life by stirring and reviving of the spirits, holding a secret sympathy with them; besides, the exercise of singing openeth the

a Deuteronomy 32.
b It was an instrument three square, of 72 strings, of incomparable sweetness.
c Answering one another in the choir.
d II Chronicles 5:12, 13.

3 Peacham's reference is not clear.
4 Exodus 15:20, 21.
5 Cf. *Epistola* LIII, 8.
6 Cf. *Epistola* LXXVII, 11: Et aurata Templorum tecta reboans.

breast and pipes. It is an enemy to melancholy and dejection of the mind, which St. Chrysostom truly calleth the Devil's bath; [e] yea, a curer of some diseases—in Apulia in Italy and thereabouts it is most certain that those who are stung with the tarantula are cured only by music. Beside the aforesaid benefit of singing, it is a most ready help for a bad pronunciation and distinct speaking which I have heard confirmed by many great divines; yea, I myself have known many children to have been holpen of their stammering in speech only by it.

Plato calleth it "a divine and heavenly practice," [f] profitable for the seeking out of that which is good and honest.

Homer saith musicians are "worthy of honor and regard of the whole world," [g] and we know, albeit Lycurgus imposed most straight and sharp laws upon the Lacedaemonians, yet he ever allowed them the exercise of music.

Aristotle averreth music to be the only disposer of the mind to virtue and goodness, wherefore he reckoneth it among those four principal exercises wherein he would have children instructed.[h]

Tully saith there consisteth in the practice of singing and playing upon instruments great knowledge and the most excellent instruction of the mind, and for the effect it worketh in the mind he termeth it "Stabilem thesaurum, qui mores instuit, componitque, ac mollit irarum ardores, &c."; a lasting treasure which rectifieth and ordereth our manners and allayeth the heat and fury of our anger, &c.[i]

I might run into an infinite sea of the praise and use of so excellent an art, but I only show it you with the finger, because I desire not that any noble or gentleman should (save at his private recreation and leisurable hours) prove a master in the same or neglect his more weighty employments, though I avouch it a skill worthy the knowledge and exercise of the greatest prince.

King Henry the Eighth could not only sing his part sure, but of himself composed a service of four, five, and six parts, as Erasmus in a certain epistle testifieth of his own knowledge.[j]

The Duke of Venosa, an Italian prince,[v] in like manner of late years hath given excellent proof of his knowledge and love to music, having himself composed many rare songs which I have seen.

But above others, who carrieth away the palm for excellency, not only in music, but in whatsoever is to be wished in a brave prince, is the yet

---

e *In lib. de Angore animi.*
f Δαιμόνιον πρᾶγμα.—*Republic,* 531C.
g Τιμῆς ἔμμοροί εἰσι καὶ αἰδοῦς.—*Odyssey,* VIII, 480.
h *Politics,* 1337B (*S.R.* I, 14).

i Cicero, *Tusculan Disputations,* I. [Peacham's reference is not correct.—Ed.]
j In *Farragine Epistola.*
v Carlo Gesualdo, Prince of Venosa.

living Maurice, Landgrave of Hesse, of whose own composition I have seen eight or ten several sets of motets and solemn music, set purposely for his own chapel, where, for the great honor of some festival and many times for his recreation only, he is his own organist. Besides he readily speaketh ten or twelve several languages, he is so universal a scholar that, coming (as he doth often) to his University of Marburg, what questions soever he meeteth with set up (as the manner is in the German and our universities), he will extempore dispute an hour or two (even in boots and spurs) upon them with their best professors. I pass over his rare skill in chirurgy, he being generally accounted the best bone-setter in the country. Who have seen his estate, his hospitality, his rich furnished armory, his grave stable of great horses, his courtesy to all strangers, being men of quality and good parts, let them speak the rest.

But since the natural inclination of some men driveth them as it were perforce to the top of excellency, examples of this kind are very rare; yea, great personages many times are more violently carried than might well stand with their honors and necessity of their affairs. Yet were it to these honest and commendable exercises, savoring of virtue, it were well; but many, neglecting their duties and places, will addict themselves wholly to trifles and the most ridiculous and childish practices. As Eropus, King of Macedonia, took pleasure only in making of candies,[k] Domitian his recreation was to catch and kill flies, and could not be spoken with many times in so serious employment.[l] Ptolomaeus Philadelphus was an excellent smith and a basket-maker, Alphonse Atestino, Duke of Ferrara, delighted himself only in turning and playing the joiner, Rodolph, the late emperor, in setting of stones and making watches. Which and the like much eclipse state and majesty, bringing familiarity and by consequence contempt with the meanest. I desire no more in you than to sing your part sure and at the first sight, withal to play the same upon your viol, or the exercise of the lute privately to yourself.

To deliver you my opinion, whom among other authors you should imitate and allow for the best, there being so many equally good, is somewhat difficult; yet as in the rest herein you shall have my opinion.

For motets and music of piety and devotion, as well for the honor of our nation as the merit of the man, I prefer above all others our phoenix, Mr. William Byrd, whom in that kind I know not whether any may equal, I am sure none excel, even by the judgment of France and Italy,

---

k Cuspinianus, *De Caesaribus et Imperatoribus.*   l Suetonius, *Lives of the Caesars*, VIII.

who are very sparing in the commendation of strangers in regard of that conceit they hold of themselves. His *Cantiones sacrae*,[8] as also his *Gradualia*,[9] are mere angelical and divine, and being of himself naturally disposed to gravity and piety his vein is not so much for light madrigals or canzonets, yet his "Virginelle" [10] and some others in his First Set cannot be mended by the best Italian of them all.

For composition I prefer next Ludovico de Victoria, a most judicious and a sweet composer; after him Orlando di Lasso, a very rare and excellent author who lived some forty years since in the court of the Duke of Bavaria. He hath published as well in Latin as French many sets; his vein is grave and sweet; among his Latin songs his *Seven Penitential Psalms* are the best, and that French set of his wherein is "Susanna un jour," [11] upon which ditty many others have since exercised their invention.[12]

For delicious air and sweet invention in madrigals, Luca Marenzio excelleth all other whosoever, having published more sets than any author else whosoever, and to say truth hath not an ill song, though sometime an oversight (which might be the printer's fault) of two eights or fifths escaped him, as between the tenor and bass in the last close of "I must depart all hapless," ending according to the nature of the ditty most artificially with a minim rest. His first, second, and third parts of "Tirsi," "Veggo dolce mio bene," "Che fa hogg'il mio sole," "Cantava," or "Sweet singing Amaryllis," are songs the muses themselves might not have been ashamed to have had composed.[13] Of stature and complexion he was a little and black man; he was organist in the Pope's chapel at Rome a good while; afterward he went into Poland, being in displeasure with the Pope for overmuch familiarity with a kinswoman of his (whom the Queen of Poland sent for by Luca Marenzio afterward, she being one of the rarest women in Europe for her voice and the lute). But returning, he found the affection of the Pope so estranged from him that hereupon he took a conceit and died.

Alphonso Ferabosco the father, while he lived, for judgment and depth of skill (as also his son yet living) was inferior unto none; what

8 *Collected Vocal Works*, I–III (London, 1937).

9 *Tudor Church Music*, VII (Oxford, 1927); *Collected Vocal Works*, IV–VII (London, 1938).

10 *The English Madrigal School* (London, 1920), XIV, No. 44 and 45; the words are translated from Ariosto.

11 *Works*, XIV, No. 64.

12 Cf. the settings by Ferabosco (*The Old English Edition*, XI, No. 1), Byrd (*The English Madrigal School*, XIV, No. 29, and XV, No. 8), Sweelinck (*Works*, VII, No. 8), and Farnaby (*The English Madrigal School*, XX, No. 12).

13 "Io partirò" ("I must depart all hapless"), "Tirsi," "Che fa hogg'il mio sole," and "Cantava" are reprinted in *Publikationen älterer Musik*, IV, i. The first three of these madrigals appeared with English text in Yonge's *Musica Transalpina* (1588); "Cantava" and "Veggo dolce mio bene" appeared in Watson's *Italian Madrigals Englished* (1590). The parallel fifths at the end of "Io partirò" occur in Yonge's reprint but not in the original composition.

he did was most elaborate and profound and pleasing enough in air, though Master Thomas Morley censureth him otherwise.[14] That of his, "I saw my lady weeping," [15] and the "Nightingale" (upon which ditty Master Byrd and he in a friendly emulation exercised their invention), [16] cannot be bettered for sweetness of air or depth of judgment.

I bring you now mine own master, Horatio Vecchi of Modena, beside goodness of air most pleasing of all other for his conceit and variety, wherewith all his works are singularly beautified, as well his madrigals of five and six as those his canzonets, printed at Nuremberg, wherein for trial sing his "Vivo in fuoco amoroso, Lucretia mia," where upon "Io catenato moro" with excellent judgment he driveth a crotchet through many minims, causing it to resemble a chain with the links. Again, in "S'io potessi raccor'i mei sospiri," the breaking of the word "sospiri" with crotchet and crotchet rest into sighs, and that "Fa mi un canzone, &c.," to make one sleep at noon, with sundry other of like conceit and pleasant invention.[17]

Then that great master, and master not long since of St. Mark's chapel in Venice,[m] second to none for a full, lofty, and sprightly vein, following none save his own humor, who while he lived was one of the most free and brave companions of the world. His *Penitential Psalms* are excellently composed and for piety are his best.

Nor must I here forget our rare countryman Peter Philips, organist to their Altezzas at Brussels, now one of the greatest masters of music in Europe. He hath sent us over many excellent songs, as well motets as madrigals; he affecteth altogether the Italian vein.

There are many other authors very excellent, as Boschetto [n] and Claudio de Monteverdi, equal to any before named, Giovanni Ferretti, Stephano Felis, Giulio Rinaldi, Philippe de Monte, Andrea Gabrieli, Cipriano de Rore, Pallavicino, Geminiano, with others yet living, whose several works for me here to examine would be over tedious and needless; and for me, please your own ear and fancy. Those whom I have before mentioned have been ever (within these thirty or forty years) held for the best.

I willingly, to avoid tediousness, forbear to speak of the worth and excellency of the rest of our English composers, Master Doctor Dowland,

m Giovanni Croce.

n Boschetto, his motets of 8 parts printed in Rome, 1594.

14 *A Plain and Easy Introduction*, p. 180 (p. 85 above).

15 *The Old English Edition*, XI, No. 2 and 3.

16 Ferabosco's setting is reprinted in *The Old English Edition*, XI, No. 9, Byrd's in *The English Madrigal School*, XV, No. 9; both are prompted by the Lassus chanson "Le rossignol" (*Works*, XIV, No. 82), printed with English text in Yonge's *Musica Transalpina* (1588).

17 Vecchi's "Fa mi un canzone" (properly "Fa una canzone") is reprinted in Alfred Einstein, *The Italian Madrigal* (Princeton, 1949), III, No. 87. It has this refrain:

Falla d'un tuono ch'invita al dormire,
Dolcemente facendola finire.

Thomas Morley, Mr. Alphonso, Mr. Wilbye, Mr. Kirbye, Mr. Weelkes, Michael East, Mr. Bateson, Mr. Deering, with sundry others, inferior to none in the world (however much soever the Italian attributes to himself) for depth of skill and richness of conceit.

Infinite is the sweet variety that the theorique of music exerciseth the mind withal, as the contemplation of proportion, of concords and discords, diversity of moods and tones, infiniteness of invention, &c. But I dare affirm there is no one science in the world that so affecteth the free and generous spirit with a more delightful and inoffensive recreation or better disposeth the mind to what is commendable and virtuous.

The commonwealth of the Cynethenses in Arcadia, falling from the delight they formerly had in music, grew into seditious humors and civil wars, which Polybius took especially note of,[o] and I suppose hereupon it was ordained in Arcadia that everyone should practise music by the space of thirty years.

The ancient Gauls in like manner (whom Julian [p] termed barbarous) became most courteous and tractable by the practise of music.

Yea, in my opinion no rhetoric more persuadeth or hath greater power over the mind; nay, hath not music her figures, the same which rhetoric? What is a revert but her antistrophe? her reports, but sweet anaphoras? her counterchange of points, antimetaboles? her passionate airs, but prosopopoeias? with infinite other of the same nature.

How doth music amaze us when of sound discords she maketh the sweetest harmony? And who can show us the reason why two basins, bowls, brass pots, or the like, of the same bigness, the one being full, the other empty, shall stricken be a just diapason in sound one to the other; or that there should be such sympathy in sounds that two lutes of equal size being laid upon a table and tuned unison, or alike in the Gamma, G *sol re ut*, or any other string, the one stricken, the other untouched shall answer it?

But to conclude, if all arts hold their esteem and value according to their effects, account this goodly science not among the number of those which Lucian placeth without the gates of hell as vain and unprofitable, but of such which are πηγαὶ τῶν καλῶν, the fountains of our lives' good and happiness. Since it is a principal means of glorifying our merciful Creator, it heightens our devotion, it gives delight and ease to our travails, it expelleth sadness and heaviness of spirit, preserveth people in concord and amity, allayeth fierceness and anger, and lastly, is the best physic for many melancholy diseases.

---

o *Histories*, IV. xx (quoted by Athenaeus,   p *Epistola 71* (Hertlein).
S.R. I, 51).

III

Reformation and Counter-Reformation

17. Martin Luther

The great German reformer was born at Eisleben in 1483 and died there in 1546. From 1522 on, a great deal of his attention was directed toward achieving a reform of the services of the church. Luther had long occupied himself with the idea of a German Mass, and during 1524 he worked on the realization of this project, assisted by two musical collaborators, Johann Walther and Conrad Rupff. The result of these efforts was the publication of Luther's "German Mass." At the same time, the reformer was turning his attention to writing and adapting hymns to be sung during the service. The Wittemberg Gesangbuch, which also appeared in 1524, has remained to our day the basis of the musical part of the service of the Evangelical church. And yet, none of the tunes introduced into Protestant church singing can be attributed to Luther himself with any degree of certainty, not even the most famous of them, "Ein' feste Burg ist unser Gott."

Wittemberg Gesangbuch [1]

[*1524*]

Foreword to the first edition

THAT THE singing of spiritual songs is a good thing and one pleasing to God is, I believe, not hidden from any Christian, for not only the example of the prophets and kings in the Old Testament (who praised God with singing and playing, with hymns and the sound of all manner of stringed instruments), but also the special custom of singing psalms, have been known to everyone and to universal Christianity from the beginning. Nay, St. Paul establishes this also, I Corinthians 14, and orders

---

1 Text: *Publikationen aelterer praktischer und theoretischer Musikwerke.* VII (Berlin, 1878), preceding p 1 of score

the Colossians to sing psalms and spiritual songs to the Lord in their hearts, in order that God's word and Christ's teaching may be thus spread abroad and practised in every way.

Accordingly, as a good beginning and to encourage those who can do better, I and several others have brought together certain spiritual songs with a view to spreading abroad and setting in motion the holy Gospel which now, by the grace of God, has again emerged, so that we too may pride ourselves, as Moses does in his song, Exodus 15, that Christ is our strength and song and may not know anything to sing or to say, save Jesus Christ our Savior, as Paul says, I Corinthians 2.

These, further, are set for four voices for no other reason than that I wished that the young (who, apart from this, should and must be trained in music and in other proper arts) might have something to rid them of their love ditties and wanton songs and might, instead of these, learn wholesome things and thus yield willingly, as becomes them, to the good; also, because I am not of the opinion that all the arts shall be crushed to earth and perish through the Gospel, as some bigoted persons pretend, but would willingly see them all, and especially music, servants of Him who gave and created them. So I pray that every pious Christian may bear with this and, should God grant him an equal or a greater talent, help to further it. Besides, unfortunately, the world is so lax and so forgetful in training and teaching its neglected young people that one might well encourage this first of all. God grant us His grace. Amen.

18. Johann Walther

Luther's friend and musical adviser, Johann Walther was born in 1496 and died in 1570 at Torgau, where he had become a choir singer to the Elector of Saxony in 1524 and choirmaster in 1525. He was sent to Dresden in 1548 and remained there until 1554 but subsequently returned to his home.

Walther assisted Luther in working out the musical part of the German Protestant Mass and the Wittemberg Gesangbuch. He published several collections of polyphonic church songs, and other compositions of his are found in various miscellaneous collections published by German music publishers of the sixteenth century.

Wittemberg Gesangbuch [1]

[1537]

Foreword to the revised edition

No WONDER that music is so utterly despised and rejected at this time, seeing that other arts, which after all we should and must possess, are so lamentably regarded by everyone as altogether worthless. But the Devil will have his way: now that, by the grace of God, we have overthrown against him the popish mass with all its trappings, he throws to the ground in turn, as best he can, all that God requires. Yet, in order that our fair art may not be thus wholly destroyed, I have—in God's praise and in pure defiance of the Devil and his contempt—brought out in print the spiritual songs formerly printed at Wittemberg, setting the greater part anew, insofar as God permitted me, carefully correcting and improving the rest, and further adding several little pieces for five and

---

1 Text: With Luther's foreword (see above).

six voices. So I pray that every pious Christian may bear with this my insufficiency and do the same or better for the glory of God and the furtherance of the art. And although these my songs will have many critics, I readily concede to anyone the honor of being my judge, seeing that I perhaps am still a student in this art. With this I commend all pious Christians to almighty God; may He grant us all his grace. Amen.

19. Jean Calvin

Jean Calvin (or Cauvin), the great Franco-Swiss religious reformer, was born at Noyon, France, in 1509, and died at Geneva in 1564. He lived first in Paris but was forced to leave because of his leanings toward the cause of reformation. He fled to Basle in 1534 and published in that city his *Institutio religionis christianae* (1536). Subsequently Calvin settled and taught in Geneva, where he spent the rest of his life building up a church community in accordance with his religious convictions. Here the French translation of the Psalter by Marot and Bèze, which was to assume such importance for the service of the Calvinist Church, was published in 1543.

Geneva Psalter [1]

[*1543*]

Foreword

THE EPISTLE TO THE READER

JEAN CALVIN to all Christians and lovers of God's Word, Salutation:

As it is a thing indeed demanded by Christianity, and one of the most necessary, that each of the faithful observe and maintain the communion of the Church in his neighborhood, attending the assemblies which are held both on the Lord's day and on other days to honor and serve God, so it is also expedient and reasonable that all should know and hear what is said and done in the temple, to receive fruit and edification therefrom. For our Lord did not institute the order which we must observe when we gather together in His name merely that the world might be amused by seeing and looking upon it, but wished rather that therefrom should

---

1 Text: *Oeuvres choisies. Publiées par la Compagnie des pasteurs de Genève* (Geneva, 1909), pp. 169-170, 173-176.

come profit to all His people. Thus witnesseth Saint Paul,[2] commanding that all which is done in the Church be directed unto the common edifying of all, a thing the servant would not have commanded, had it not been the intention of the Master. For to say that we can have devotion, either at prayers or at ceremonies, without understanding anything of them, is a great mockery, however much it be commonly said. A good affection toward God is not a thing dead and brutish, but a lively movement, proceeding from the Holy Spirit when the heart is rightly touched and the understanding enlightened. And indeed, if one could be edified by the things which one sees without knowing what they mean, Saint Paul would not so rigorously forbid speaking in an unknown tongue and would not use the argument that where there is no doctrine, there is no edification.[3] Yet if we wish to honor well the holy decrees of our Lord, as used in the Church, the main thing is to know what they contain, what they mean, and to what end they tend, in order that their observance may be useful and salutary and in consequence rightly ruled.

Now there are in brief three things that our Lord has commanded us to observe in our spiritual assemblies, namely, the preaching of His Word, the public and solemn prayers, and the administration of His sacraments. I abstain at this time from speaking of preaching, seeing that there is no question thereof. . . . Of the sacraments I shall speak later.

As to the public prayers, these are of two kinds: some are offered by means of words alone, the others with song. And this is not a thing invented a little time ago, for it has existed since the first origin of the Church; this appears from the histories, and even Saint Paul speaks not only of praying by word of mouth, but also of singing.[4] And in truth we know by experience that song has great force and vigor to move and inflame the hearts of men to invoke and praise God with a more vehement and ardent zeal. It must always be looked to that the song be not light and frivolous but have weight and majesty, as Saint Augustine says,[5] and there is likewise a great difference between the music one makes to entertain men at table and in their homes, and the psalms which are sung in the Church in the presence of God and His angels.

Therefore, when anyone wishes to judge rightly of the form that is here presented, we hope that he will find it holy and pure, for it is entirely directed toward that edification of which we have spoken, however more widely the practice of singing may extend. For even in our homes and in the fields it should be an incentive, and as it were an organ

2 1 Corinthians 14:26.
3 1 Corinthians 14:19.
4 1 Corinthians 14:15.
5 Cf. *Epistola* LV, xviii, 34.

for praising God and lifting up our hearts to Him, to console us by medi-
tating upon His virtue, goodness, wisdom, and justice, a thing more necessary than one can say. In the first place, it is not without reason that the
Holy Spirit exhorts us so carefully by means of the Holy Scripture to
rejoice in God and that all our joy is there reduced to its true end, for
He knows how much we are inclined to delight in vanity. Just as our
nature, then, draws us and induces us to seek all means of foolish and
vicious rejoicing, so, to the contrary, our Lord, to distract us and withdraw us from the enticements of the flesh and the world, presents to
us all possible means in order to occupy us in that spiritual joy which
He so much recommends to us.[6] Now among the other things proper
to recreate man and give him pleasure, music is either the first or one of
the principal, and we must think that it is a gift of God deputed to that
purpose. For which reason we must be the more careful not to abuse it,
for fear of soiling and contaminating it, converting it to our condemna-
tion when it has been dedicated to our profit and welfare. Were there
no other consideration than this alone, it might well move us to moderate
the use of music to make it serve all that is of good repute and that it
should not be the occasion of our giving free rein to dissoluteness or of
our making ourselves effeminate with disordered pleasures and that it
should not become the instrument of lasciviousness or of any shameless-
ness. But there is still more, for there is hardly anything in the world with
more power to turn or bend, this way and that, the morals of men, as
Plato has prudently considered.[7] And in fact we find by experience that
it has a secret and almost incredible power to move our hearts in one
way or another.

Wherefore we must be the more diligent in ruling it in such a manner
that it may be useful to us and in no way pernicious. For this reason the
early doctors of the Church often complain that the people of their times
are addicted to dishonest and shameless songs, which not without reason
they call mortal and Satanic poison for the corruption of the world. Now
in speaking of music I understand two parts, namely, the letter, or subject and matter, and the song, or melody. It is true that, as Saint Paul
says, every evil word corrupts good manners,[8] but when it has the melody
with it, it pierces the heart much more strongly and enters within; as
wine is poured into the cask with a funnel, so venom and corruption are
distilled to the very depths of the heart by melody. Now what is there
to do? It is to have songs not merely honest but also holy, which will be

---

6 Here ends the preface in the first edition
(1542). What follows is found only in the edition
of 1545 and in those of the Psalter. [Choisy]

7 *Republic,* 401D (*S.R.* I, 8).
8 Ephesians 4:29.

like spurs to incite us to pray to God and praise Him, and to meditate upon His works in order to love, fear, honor, and glorify Him. Now what Saint Augustine says is true—that no one can sing things worthy of God save what he has received from Him.[9] Wherefore, although we look far and wide and search on every hand, we shall not find better songs nor songs better suited to that end than the Psalms of David which the Holy Spirit made and uttered through him. And for this reason, when we sing them we may be certain that God puts the words in our mouths as if Himself sang in us to exalt His glory. Wherefore Chrysostom exhorts men as well as women and little children to accustom themselves to sing them, in order that this may be like a meditation to associate them with the company of angels.[10] Then we must remember what Saint Paul says—that spiritual songs cannot be well sung save with the heart.[11] Now the heart requires the intelligence, and therein, says Saint Augustine, lies the difference between the singing of men and of birds.[12] For a linnet, a nightingale, a parrot will sing well, but it will be without understanding. Now the peculiar gift of man is to sing knowing what he is saying. After the intelligence must follow the heart and the affection, which cannot be unless we have the hymn imprinted on our memory in order never to cease singing.

For these reasons the present book, even for this cause, besides the rest which has been said, should be in singular favor with everyone who desires to enjoy himself honestly and in God's way, that is, for his welfare and to the profit of his neighbors, and thus it has no need to be much recommended by me, seeing that it carries its value and its praise. But may the world be so well advised that instead of the songs that it has previously used, in part vain and frivolous, in part stupid and dull, in part foul and vile and consequently evil and harmful, it may accustom itself hereafter to sing these divine and celestial hymns with the good King David. Touching the melody, it has seemed best that it be moderated in the way that we have adopted in order that it may have the weight and majesty proper to the subject and may even be suitable for singing in Church, according to what has been said.

Geneva, June 10, 1543.

---

9 *In Psalmum XXXIV Enarratio*, I, 1.
10 *Exposition of Psalm XLI* (S.R. I, 68–70).
11 Ephesians 5:19.
12 *In Psalmum XVIII Enarratio*, II, 1.

20. Claude Goudimel

Born at Besançon circa 1505, Goudimel lost his life in 1572 as a victim of the Huguenot massacres at Lyon. His first compositions are found in the extensive collections of French chansons published in 1549 by Nicolas du Chemin in Paris. In 1557 and 1558 Goudimel published a Magnificat and four masses—his last music for the services of the Catholic Church. In all, Goudimel published three distinct settings of the tunes in the Huguenot psalters—one in motet-style between 1551 and 1566, and two for four voices, simply harmonized, in 1564 and 1565.

Geneva Psalter [1]

[1565]

Foreword to the edition of 1565

To our readers:

To the melody of the psalms we have, in this little volume, adapted three parts, not to induce you to sing them in Church, but that you may rejoice in God, particularly in your homes. This should not be found an ill thing, the more so since the melody used in Church is left in its entirety, just as though it were alone.

1 Text: The facsimile of the original edition (Geneva, 1565), published by the Bärenreiter-Verlag (Cassel, 1935).

21. Thomas Cranmer

An English churchman and one of the principal promoters of Reformation in his native country, Cranmer was born in 1489. He was appointed Chaplain to Henry VIII and became Archbishop of Canterbury in 1533. Cranmer played an important role in the early history of the Church of England, particularly in the publishing of the Book of Common Prayer. He died at the stake as a heretic in 1556, during Mary's reign.

Letter to Henry VIII [1]

[1544]

IT MAY please Your Majesty to be advertised that, according to Your Highness' commandment, sent unto me by Your Grace's secretary, Mr. Pagett, I have translated into the English tongue, so well as I could in so short time, certain processions to be used upon festival days if after due correction and amendment of the same Your Highness shall think it so convenient. In which translation, forasmuch as many of the processions in the Latin were but barren, as meseemed, and little fruitful, I was constrained to use more than the liberty of a translator: for in some processions I have altered divers words; in some I have added part; in some taken part away; some I have left out whole, either for because the matter appeared to me to be little to purpose, or because the days be not with us festival days; and some processions I have added whole because I thought I had a better matter for the purpose than was the procession in Latin. The judgment whereof I refer wholly unto Your Majesty, and after Your Highness hath corrected it, if Your Grace command some devout and solemn note to be made thereunto (as it is

1 Text: *Miscellaneous Writings and Letters* (Cambridge, 1846), p. 412.

to the procession which Your Majesty hath already set forth in English) [2] I trust it will much excitate and stir the hearts of all men unto devotion and godliness. But in my opinion, the song that should be made thereunto would not be full of notes, but, as near as may be, for every syllable a note, so that it may be sung distinctly and devoutly as be in the matins and evensong Venite, the hymns, Te Deum, Benedictus, Magnificat, Nunc dimittis, and all the psalms and versicles; and in the mass Gloria in excelsis, Gloria Patri, the Creed, the Preface, the Pater Noster, and some of the Sanctus and Agnus. As concerning the "Salva festa dies," the Latin note, as I think, is sober and distinct enough, wherefore I have travailed to make the verses in English and have put the Latin note unto the same. Nevertheless, they that be cunning in singing can make a much more solemn note thereto. I made them only for a proof, to see how English would do in song.[3] But because mine English verses lack the grace and facility that I wish they had, Your Majesty may cause some other to make them again that can do the same in more pleasant English and phrase. As for the sentence, I suppose will serve well enough. Thus Almighty God preserve Your Majesty in long and prosperous health and felicity!

From Bekisbourne, the 7th of October.
    Your Grace's most bounden
      chaplain and beadsman,
        T. Cantuarien

To the King's most excellent Majesty

---

2 *An Exhortation unto Prayer* (London, Richard Grafton, June 16, 1544). The full title continues: "Thought meet by the King's Majesty and his clergy to be read to the people in every church afore processions. Also a litany with suffrages to be said or sung in the time of the said processions."

3 Cranmer's translation seems not to have been published or preserved.

22. Thomas East

An important typographer and publisher, Thomas East (or Easte, Este), is remembered as the publisher of much Elizabethan music. Between 1588 and 1607, he printed a long series of works by Byrd, Yonge, Watson, Morley, Kirbye, Wilbye, Dowland, Jones, and other authors. His first publication was William Byrd's *Psalms, Sonnets and Songs of Sadness and Piety*. In 1592 he edited *The Whole Book of Psalms, With Their Wonted Tunes, in Four Parts*. Two other editions appeared in 1594 and 1604. This collection was one of the first to appear in score, rather than in separate part-books.

The Whole Book of Psalms [1]

[*1592*]

Dedication and preface

To the Right Honorable Sir John Puckering, Knight, Lord Keeper of the Great Seal of England:

The word of God, Right Honorable, delighteth those which are spiritually minded; the art of music recreateth such as are not sensually affected; where zeal in the one and skill in the other do meet, the whole man is revived. The mercies of God are great provoking unto thankfulness; the necessities of man are great, enforcing unto prayer; the state of us all is such that the publishing of God's glory for the edifying one of another cannot be overslipped; in all these the heart must be the workmaster, the tongue the instrument, and a sanctified knowledge as the hand to polish the work. The Psalms of David are a paraphrasis of

---

1 The original edition (London, 1592). A reprint, edited by E. F. Rimbault, was published in 1844 as Vol. 11 of the series brought out by the Musical Antiquarian Society.

the Scriptures; they teach us thankfulness, prayer, and all the duties of a Christian whatsoever; they have such comfort in them that such as will be conversant in the same cannot possibly lose their labor. Blessed is that man which delighteth therein and meditateth in the same continually. He that is heavy hath the Psalms to help his prayer; he that is merry hath the Psalms to guide his affections; and he that hath a desire to be seriously employed in either of these duties hath this excellent gift of God, the knowledge of music, offered him for his further help; that the heart rejoicing in the word and the ears delighting in the notes and tunes, both these might join together unto the praise of God. Some have pleased themselves with pastorals, others with madrigals, but such as are endued with David's heart desire with David to sing unto God psalms and hymns and spiritual songs. For whose sake I have set forth this work that they busy themselves in the psalms of this holy man, being by men of skill put into four parts that each man may sing that part which best may serve his voice.

In this book the church tunes are carefully corrected and other short tunes added which are sung in London and other places of this realm. And regarding chiefly to help the simple, curiosity is shunned. The profit is theirs that will use this book; the pains theirs that have compiled it; the charges his who, setting it forth, respecteth a public benefit, not his private gain. Now having finished it, in most humble manner I present it unto Your Honor as to a maintainer of godliness, a friend to virtue, and a lover of music, hoping of Your Lordship's favorable acceptance, craving your honorable patronage and countenance, and praying unto God long to continue Your Lordship a protector of the just and the same God to be a protector of Your Lordship's welfare forever.

Your good Lordship's most humbly at command

Thomas East.

The Preface

Although I might have used the skill of some one learned musician in the setting of these psalms in four parts, yet for variety's sake I have entreated the help of many, being such as I know to be expert in the art and sufficient to answer such curious carping musicians whose skill hath not been employed to the furthering of this work.[2] And I have not only set down in this book all the tunes usually printed heretofore with as

2 East's contributors were John Farmer, George Kirbye, Richard Allison, Giles Farnaby, Edward Blancks, John Dowland, William Cob-bold, Edmund Hooper, Edward Johnson, and Michael Cavendish.

much truth as I could possibly gather among divers of our ordinary psalm books, but also have added those which are commonly sung nowadays and not printed in our common psalm books with the rest. And all this have I so orderly cast that the four parts lie always together in open sight. The which my travail, as it hath been to the furtherance of music in all Godly sort and to the comfort of all good Christians, so I pray thee to take it in good part and use it to the glory of God.

T. E.

23. Jacob de Kerle

Born at Ypres, Belgium, in 1531, de Kerle died in 1591 at Prague. He was first organist or choirmaster at Orvieto in Italy, later in Bavaria, and subsequently in Ypres, Rome, Augsburg, Cambrai, and Cologne. From 1582 until his death he was court chaplain to Rudolph II.

De Kerle's biography is varied and interesting because of the important political and religious events in which he took part. The style of his music is elaborately polyphonic; at times he uses also the new devices of contemporary chromaticism. De Kerle left works in the different forms of religious music but did not altogether neglect madrigal writing. His *Preces speciales,* written for the Council of Trent, were published at Venice in 1562.

Preces speciales [1]

[*1562*]

Dedication

To the Most Illustrious and Reverend Lords Ercole Cardinal of
Mantua, Girolamo Cardinal Seripando, Stanislaus Cardinal
of Ermland, Lodovico Cardinal Simonetta, Mark Cardinal of Hohenems, Legates of the Tridentine
Council, His Most Worshipful Lords

THESE TEN forms of pious prayer under the title of responses, by Pietro Soto, a member of the Dominican Order and a man of apostolic life and doctrine, and accommodated to the figures and modes of music by me at the command of that best and most distinguished prince the Cardinal Bishop of Augsburg, my patron, I have thought best to send to you,

1 Text: *Denkmäler der Tonkunst in Bayern,* XXVI (Augsburg, 1926), lxviii.

165

most wise and illustrious Fathers, who preside over the public council of the Christian Church. For since whatever time remains free from the salutary affairs of the Republic you devote to divine matters and sacred offices, I have hoped that these prayers, not unrelated either to the praises of God or to the time of the Church, would not be displeasing to you. You will not, I think, reject the plan of joining musical numbers to these prayers, a plan which that most holy man David, the man after God's own heart, employed. If you less approve my own skill in the matter, you will surely not disapprove of my purpose; for what I can, I contribute to the glory of God in the sight of all. For if God judges the services and works of men not by the weight of the matter but by their minds, then the nearer to God you approach than other men, the more you are wishing to imitate His benignity. Oh, that it may only be possible for us to call down the mercy of God by pious prayers as we perceive is done by your wise actions! Given at Rome.

Your Most Illustrious and Reverend Lordships'
Most Humble and Devoted Servant,
Jacobus de Kerle

24. Pope Gregory XIII

The brief of Gregory XIII, entrusting Palestrina and his colleague Annibale Zoilo with the revision of the music of the Roman Gradual and Antiphoner, was a natural outgrowth of the publication, in 1568 and 1570, of the reformed Breviary and Missal ordered by the Council of Trent and approved by Gregory's predecessor, Paul V. The aim of this proposed revision was twofold: on the one hand, it was to bring the choir books into agreement with the liturgical revisions already made official; on the other, it was to rid the plainsong melodies of those "barbarisms, obscurities, contrarieties, and superfluities" which were offensive to Renaissance sensibilities. During the year 1578, as his correspondence shows, Palestrina was deeply preoccupied with this work of revision; later on, however, he seems to have set it aside, never to take it up again. In 1611, some years after his death, other hands were charged with the responsibility, and although it seems clear that the so-called "Editio Medicaea," published in 1614, is not very different from the revised version that Palestrina must have had in mind, it is on the whole unlikely that it actually includes any work of his.

Pope from 1572 to 1585, Gregory XIII (Ugo Buoncompagno) inaugurated important changes in the musical arrangements at St. Peter's. His revision of the calendar has made his name a household word. To him Palestrina dedicated his Fourth Book of Masses (1582) and his motets on the Song of Solomon (Book V, 1584).

Brief on the Reform of the Chant [1]

[*October 25, 1577*]

To Palestrina and Zoilo

BELOVED SONS:

Greetings and apostolic benediction!

Inasmuch as it has come to our attention that the Antiphoners, Graduals, and Psalters that have been provided with music for the celebration of the divine praises and offices in plainsong (as it is called) since the publication of the Breviary and Missal ordered by the Council of Trent have been filled to overflowing with barbarisms, obscurities, contrarieties, and superfluities as a result of the clumsiness or negligence or even wickedness of the composers, scribes, and printers: in order that these books may agree with the aforesaid Breviary and Missal, as is appropriate and fitting, and may at the same time be so ordered, their superfluities having been shorn away and their barbarisms and obscurities removed, that through their agency God's name may be reverently, distinctly, and devoutly praised; desiring to provide for this in so far as with God's help we may, we have decided to turn to you, whose skill in the art of music and in singing, whose faithfulness and diligence, and whose piety toward God have been fully tested, and to assign to you this all-important task, trusting confidently that you will amply satisfy this desire of ours. And thus we charge you with the business of revising and (so far as shall seem expedient to you) of purging, correcting, and reforming these Antiphoners, Graduals, and Psalters, together with such other chants as are used in our churches according to the rite of Holy Roman Church, whether at the Canonical Hours or at Mass or at other divine services, and over all of these things we entrust you for the present with full and unrestricted jurisdiction and power by virtue of our apostolic authority, and in order that you may pursue the aforesaid more quickly and diligently you have our permission to admit other skilled musicians as as-

---

[1] Text: Raphael Molitor, *Die nach-Tridentinische Choral-Reform zu Rom*, I (Leipzig, 1901), 297–298.

sistants if you so desire. The Apostolic Constitutions and any other regulations that may be to the contrary notwithstanding. Given at St. Peter's in Rome under Peter's seal this twenty-fifth day of October, 1577, in the sixth year of our pontificate.

To our beloved sons Giovanni Pierluigi da Palestrina and Annibale Zoilo Romano, musicians of our private chapel.

Index

PORTAGE PUBLIC LIBRARY
300 LIBRARY LANE
PORTAGE, MI   49002

GAYLORD